VARDY

MATT AND TOM OLDFIELD

ULTIMATE
FOOTBALL HEROES

VARDY

FROM THE PLAYGROUND
TO THE PITCH

DINO

First published by Dino Books in 2021,
an imprint of Bonnier Books UK,
The Plaza, 535 King's Road, London SW10 0SZ
Owned by Bonnier Books,
Sveavägen 56, Stockholm, Sweden

@dinobooks
@footieheroesbks
www.heroesfootball.com
www.bonnierbooks.co.uk

Design by www.envydesign.co.uk

Paperback ISBN: 978 1 78946 450 4
E-book ISBN: 978 1 78946 455 9

British Library cataloguing-in-publication data:
A catalogue record for this book is available from the British Library.

Printed and bound in Great Britain by Clays Ltd, Elcograf S.p.A.

1 3 5 7 9 10 8 6 4 2

For Noah and Nico,
Southampton's future strikeforce.

ULTIMATE
FOOTBALL HEROES

Matt Oldfield is an accomplished writer and the editor-in-chief
of football review site Of Pitch & Page. Tom Oldfield is a freelance sports
writer and the author of biographies on Cristiano Ronaldo, Arsène
Wenger and Rafael Nadal.

Cover illustration by Dan Leydon.
To learn more about Dan visit danleydon.com
To purchase his artwork visit etsy.com/shop/footynews
Or just follow him on Twitter @danleydon

TABLE OF CONTENTS

ACKNOWLEDGEMENTS

First of all, I'd like to thank Bonnier Books UK for supporting me throughout and for running the ever-expanding UFH ship so smoothly. Writing stories for the next generation of football fans is both an honour and a pleasure.

I wouldn't be doing this if it wasn't for Tom. I owe him so much and I'm very grateful for his belief in me as an author. I feel like Robin setting out on a solo career after a great partnership with Batman. I hope I do him (Tom, not Batman) justice with these new books.

Next up, I want to thank my friends for keeping me sane during long hours in front of the laptop. Pang,

Will, Mills, Doug, John, Charlie – the laughs and the cups of coffee are always appreciated.

I've already thanked my brother but I'm also very grateful to the rest of my family, especially Melissa, Noah and of course Mum and Dad. To my parents, I owe my biggest passions: football and books. They're a real inspiration for everything I do.

Finally, I couldn't have done this without Iona's encouragement and understanding during long, work-filled weekends. Much love to you.

CHAPTER 1

"JAMIE VARDY'S HAVING A PARTY!"

2 May 2016

'Wake up ref, that's a blatant foul! I reckon he must be a Tottenham fan...'

'Come on, you Blues!'

For once, Jamie wasn't cheering for his team, Leicester City. No, he was cheering for Chelsea instead. And so were all his teammates, who were watching the game with him at his house. They were hoping for a huge party because if Chelsea could beat or draw with Spurs at Stamford Bridge, then Leicester would officially be crowned the new Premier League Champions.

'Premier League Champions' – unbelievable! It still sounded too good to be true. Surely, something that special couldn't happen to a club like Leicester City, and a striker like Jamie?

'Well, if this is a dream,' he told himself, 'then I don't ever want to wake up!'

At the start of the season, back in August, the newspapers had made Leicester one of the favourites for relegation. And the odds on The Foxes winning the title? A whopping 5000–1!

But the players didn't mind if others underestimated them. In fact, it only made them more determined to shock and succeed. All that really mattered was that *they* believed that Leicester City Football Club could keep improving. And they definitely did. The Foxes had won promotion from the Championship in 2014, then battled back from the verge of relegation in 2015. What next? To the players, anything seemed achievable in 2016, even winning the Premier League title.

So together, Jamie, his teammates, and their new manager, the Italian, Claudio Ranieri, had set out to prove everyone wrong. Claudio had started by making Leicester more solid and organised in defence. With Kasper Schmeichel in goal, Wes Morgan and Robert Huth at the back and little N'Golo Kanté winning every ball back in midfield, they had soon stopped conceding goals and started collecting clean sheets instead.

Excellent. And at the other end? Well, Ranieri could see that Leicester's line-up was perfect for the quick counter-attack. They had the hard work of Shinji Okazaki and Leonardo Ulloa, combined with the creativity of Riyad Mahrez, Marc Albrighton and Danny Drinkwater, and the speed and clever runs of Jamie. Oh, and the shooting too, of course…

GOAL!

GOAL!

GOAL!

In his first year in the Premier League, Jamie had only grabbed five goals all season, but he felt so much sharper second time around. All he'd needed was a bit of time to adapt, just like when he first arrived in the Championship. Now, he was ready to wear the 'Number 9' shirt with pride, as had his childhood hero, Sheffield Wednesday's David Hirst, back in the day.

Suddenly, the £1 million that Leicester had paid to sign Jamie from Fleetwood Town looked like an absolute bargain because once he started scoring, he couldn't stop. He was banging them in, week after week, against the best defences in Britain. With eleven goals in eleven consecutive games, he had even broken the Premier League record set by Manchester United's legendary striker, Ruud van Nistelrooy. Unbelievable!

Only four years earlier, at the age of twenty-four, Jamie had still been playing non-league football, while also working in a factory. But now, he was a new Premier League record holder, the hottest striker in the country, and an England international. What a football fairytale!

And thanks to his goals, Leicester were also sitting at the top of the table. One by one, Jamie's childhood dreams were coming true. So, could his club go all the way and lift the Premier League title? Most people believed such a dream to be unthinkable, but Leicester's team spirit was so strong that no one could stop them. With each hard-fought win, the impossible had started to look more and more possible:

Leicester 2 Chelsea 1,

Tottenham 0 Leicester 1,

Leicester 2 Liverpool 0,

Manchester City 1 Leicester 3...

And now, in early May 2016, they were just ninety minutes away from achieving their aim. For one night only, every Foxes player and fan all over the world was a die-hard Chelsea supporter.

'Go on, Hazard!'

'We love you, Willian!'

At half-time, however, it didn't look good for Leicester. Tottenham were leading Chelsea 2–0, thanks to goals from Harry Kane and Son Heung-Min. It certainly wasn't the loud, happy, banging house party that Jamie had been hoping for.

'Oh well, we'll just have to win the title next week at home against Everton,' he said to Wes. 'No problem, we can do that!'

But everything changed midway through the second half. Spurs started panicking, and Chelsea started playing.

First, Gary Cahill poked the ball past Hugo Lloris from a Willian corner. *2–1!*

'Yes, you legend!' Jamie screamed at the TV screen, punching the air with passion. 'Right, game on, lads!'

Chelsea still had thirty minutes left to score that crucial equaliser. It was the start of one of the longest and most nerve-wracking half hours of the Leicester players' lives.

'Yessss!' they cheered as Diego Costa dribbled into the Spurs penalty area.

'Noooo!' they groaned as he slipped on the ball.

'Yessss!' they cheered as Hazard got the ball on the left side of the box.

'Noooo!' they groaned as his cross flew just past Costa's outstretched leg.

'Noooo!' they groaned as the ball came to Ryan Mason on the edge of the Chelsea box.

'Yessss!' they cheered as he scuffed his shot straight

at Asmir Begović.

With ten minutes to go, it was still 2–1 to Tottenham. But just when Jamie was starting to think ahead to Everton, Costa turned past Toby Alderweireld and slipped the ball across to Hazard…

'Yessss!'

…who curled it first time into the top corner. *2–2!*

'Yeeeeeeeeeeeeeeeeessssssssssssssss!'

There were amazing scenes at Stamford Bridge, and at Jamie's house too. There was an almighty explosion of noise and movement. Players were shouting, crying, jumping, hugging, and drinks were flying everywhere. Because Leicester City were now only moments away from winning the league title for the first time in 132 years.

'Come on Chelsea – just keep it tight at the back now!'

Those last ten minutes were almost unbearable for Jamie and Co. but at last, the final whistle blew. It was official – Leicester City were the new Premier League…

'*Campeones! Campeones! Olé! Olé! Olé!*' the players sang as they danced around Jamie's kitchen, arm-in-arm.

Although Jamie hadn't actually played in the game, he felt like he had. In his head, he had kicked every ball, and now he was exhausted and emotional. It was a night – and a season – that he would never forget. At last, he was doing all those things that he had dreamed of as a youngster, before that heartbreaking day when his local club Sheffield Wednesday had told him he wasn't big enough to be a top striker. After that, Jamie had almost given up on the game several times, but thanks to the support of his family and friends, he had kept on going, doing what he loved most: scoring goals. And look at him now – he was a Premier League Champion!

But now wasn't the time for resting and reflecting. No, that could wait. Because Jamie's loud, happy, banging house party was only just beginning.

CHAPTER 2

HIRSTY AT HILLSBOROUGH

'Dad, can we go now?' Jamie asked again, for the hundredth time that morning. He was already dressed and ready to go, wearing the latest club shirt and a blue-and-white scarf around his neck.

'I know you're itching to get there, son, but let's have some lunch first,' Richard replied, smiling at the memory of when he had been that same, eager little boy. 'We don't want your tummy grumbling during the game, do we? Besides, kick-off's not until three – we've got ages!'

Reluctantly, Jamie took a seat at the kitchen table, but he was too excited to eat, or to sit still for long. After a few minutes, he jumped out of his chair.

'Okay, now can we go?'

'Fine!'

He had been waiting so long for this moment – all five years of his young life. Finally, his dad had decided that Jamie was old enough to go along with him to watch his beloved Sheffield Wednesday play. Well, now it would be their beloved Sheffield Wednesday, and what a day it was going to be!

The previous year, 'The Owls' had beaten Manchester United to win the League Cup and now they were fighting for the league title too. There was no doubt that Wednesday was one of the best teams in the whole of England, with quality players in every position: Chris Woods in goal, captain Nigel Pearson in defence, Chris Bart-Williams and John Sheridan in midfield, and best of all, David Hirst, their Number 9. 'Hirsty' was a goal-scoring machine, with a lethal left foot. He was so good that he had even played three times for England.

'Manchester United keep trying to buy him, but he keeps saying no,' Jamie's dad told him proudly, as they set off on their football journey. 'He's a local lad and he's not going anywhere!'

Jamie couldn't wait to watch his hero, 'Hirsty', play live – and to watch Wednesday win, of course. And at last, he would get to see inside Hillsborough! They lived less than two miles away from the stadium, so it was always there in the distance. In fact, if he was in the right spot and his dad lifted him up on his shoulders, Jamie could see the top stands from outside their house. For as long as he could remember, Hillsborough had been Jamie's dream destination – a magical place where he longed to go.

'So, what do you think?' Richard asked as they stood near the turnstiles, waiting to go in.

As he looked up and around him, Jamie was lost for words. All he could do was gawp and smile at the size of the stadium and at the thousands of supporters everywhere.

'Come on, keep hold of my hand,' his dad said as they approached the front of the queue. 'You don't want to get lost in here!'

Being outside Hillsborough had been brilliant, but being inside the ground was even better. Jamie couldn't believe what he was seeing. The pitch looked enormous and so perfectly kept, while the rows and rows of blue seats seemed never-ending.

'This way,' Richard called, leading an overwhelmed Jamie onto 'The Kop', the only part of the stadium where the Wednesday fans were still allowed to stand, packed in tightly like a tin of sardines.

Jamie could see that his dad was trying to say something to him, but he couldn't hear a word because the singing was so loud. The atmosphere was building already, and kick-off was still half an hour away.

'What?' Jamie called up, but instead of an answer, he felt two hands lift him up so that he was standing on the blue rail in front.

'Is that better?' Richard shouted in his ear.

Jamie didn't need to reply; his wide smile said it all. Before, he could only see the backs of big, tall people, but now suddenly he had the best view in the whole stadium.

'Come on, Wednesday!' he cheered wildly, feeling on top of the world.

Wednesday's opponents that day were Notts County, a team near the bottom of the table, so everyone was expecting a comfortable home win.

'With a goal or two for Hirsty!' his dad predicted.

Jamie really hoped so. Every time his hero had the ball, he felt a rush of excitement, and so did everyone else in the stadium. At the half-time whistle, however, despite all the 'Ooooh's and 'Ahhhh's of the crowd, the score was still 0–0. Wednesday were dominating the game and creating lots of chances, but they just couldn't seem to get the ball over the goal line.

'Don't worry, there's plenty of time left,' Richard reassured his son.

Jamie wasn't worried, though; he had full faith in his football heroes. They wouldn't let him down, not when he had come all the way to Hillsborough to watch them.

Wednesday's player-manager, Trevor Francis, came on as a second-half substitute, and with time running out, he curled a high cross into the box. The Notts County defenders were so busy watching the ball that they didn't spot the striker sneaking in between them

– Hirsty! His bullet of a header flew past the keeper before he could even dive. *1–0 to Wednesday!*

HURRRAAAAAAAAAYYYYYYYYYY!!!!

Wow, Jamie had never heard a roar like it, or seen adults go quite so crazy. His dad was hugging him, screaming with pure joy. Standing up there on the handrail, it felt like the stadium was actually rocking. Unbelievable!

From that first game on, there was only one thing that Jamie wanted to do when he was older – score goals for Sheffield Wednesday at Hillsborough, just like Hirsty.

CHAPTER 3

HIRSTY AT HOME

After his amazing day at Hillsborough, Jamie returned home more football obsessed than ever. Wearing his beloved Sheffield Wednesday shirt, he spent as much time as he could practising his football skills. Unsurprisingly, his mum and dad didn't want him causing chaos around the house, and so outside he went, whatever the weather. He had lots of work to do if he wanted to be the next Hirsty!

When there was no-one else around, Jamie just kicked a ball against the back gate, over and over again. Or, if he was feeling really restless and brave, he sneaked out into the shared garden to noisily recreate the great goals he'd seen his hero score on TV, much to the annoyance of the neighbours.

'Get off there! How many times have I told you? You're ruining the grass!'

Football's always more fun when you're playing with other people, though, and luckily Jamie had lots of friends who lived close by.

'Right, everyone up for a game of Wembley?' he called out, already knowing the answer to his own question. And it was his ball, so he made the rules. 'Good, so no goal-hanging, headers count double – oh, and I'm not starting in goal!'

'Me neither!' yelled Ashley.

'Me neither!' bellowed Tim.

'Fine, I'll go in first!' Ben said with a sigh, making his way slowly over to the wall of the pub car park. Sometimes, if it was busy, they played in the quieter backstreets nearby, but this was their main stadium, their Hillsborough at home.

'Ready… GO!'

Ben launched the ball high into the air to announce the start of the battle. By the time it bounced, the three players had transformed themselves into their football heroes: Paul Warhurst, Chris Waddle, and David Hirst. Yes, they were all Wednesday fans, of course! But while the others preferred Waddle, the club's new star winger, Jamie stayed loyal to his original hero. It was scoring great goals that impressed him most, not silky skills.

Ashley and Tim battled fiercely for the ball, but as usual, Jamie was the winner. Although he was the smallest and the skinniest, no-one could match his fighting spirit. Or his speed. After tapping it past Tim, he raced towards the goal.

'He's through, one on one with the keeper, Chris Woods…'

BANG!

'…and Hirsty scores –

GOOOOOOOOAAAAAAAAALLLLLLLLLL!

Jamie was soon through to the final, and he was followed by Ashley. So, who would be the Wembley champion?

Ashley was the first to reach the ball, but he didn't have it for long. Jamie flew in with a crunching tackle, knocking him down onto the car-park floor.

'Foul!' Ashley cried out, looking over at Tim, who, as the loser, was now also the referee. But after a pause for thought, Tim shook his head. 'Play on – he got the ball!'

'No way!' Ashley flung his arms around in frustration and then sat down on the gravel, giving up. He didn't even bother chasing back because there was no way he could catch Jamie; he was far too fast. It was game over – his mate was through on goal and he hardly ever missed.

BANG!

GOAL!

It was time for Jamie's favourite tongue-twister, and he never got it wrong:

'Hirsty wins it for Wednesday at Wembley!'

It was the same story every break and lunchtime in the Malin Bridge Primary playground. In class, Jamie sat there staring at the clock, counting down the minutes until he could escape outside and play. Football was all he cared about, because when he was on the attack with the ball at his feet, he felt simply unstoppable. If there were defenders between him and the goal, he just kicked it past them, knowing that he would win the race and reach it first. Then, once he was in shooting range, he could blast the ball like Hirsty – even at the age of seven.

BANG!

GOAL!

'That Jamie's got real football talent, hasn't he?' the teachers discussed in the staffroom.

'Yes, if only he would concentrate like that in the classroom!'

CHAPTER 4

WEDNESDAY AT WEMBLEY

'Okay fine, we'll do it just this once, Jamie,' Lisa agreed at last. 'But only because it's Wednesday at Wembley, okay? And I expect you to be on your best behaviour at school from now on–'

'Yes Mum, thanks – you're the best!'

Sheffield Wednesday were on fire, making it to two cup finals in one year – first, in the League Cup, where they lost 2–1 to Arsenal, and then in the FA Cup, the oldest national football competition in the world. And who were their opponents in the final? Arsenal again! It was time for revenge. The first leg had finished 1–1 (Hirsty got the goal, of course), and in those days, instead of penalties, the match went to a replay. And who had managed to get tickets for the game? Jamie's dad! So, there was no way that Jamie could go to school and miss seeing Wednesday at Wembley.

Once Jamie's mum had phoned the school to say that her son was 'sick', they got in their car and drove all the way down to Wembley. It was a long journey, and Jamie slept for most of it. By the time he woke up, they were in London and he could see the stadium in the distance. Wow, it was even bigger and better than his beloved Hillsborough!

Once they had found somewhere to park, they joined the noisy group of Wednesday fans on the slow walk to Wembley, moving like a swarm of blue and white. It didn't even matter that they were walking in the rain; Jamie was so excited that he thought he might burst. Sheffield Wednesday were in the FA Cup Final and he would be there to watch them win! He couldn't wait to tell all his friends about it; they'd be so jealous.

The next few minutes were a blur of sound and movement as Jamie's parents led him through the heaving crowds, past the turnstiles, and up to their seats. As he sat down and looked around, Jamie experienced a feeling of awe once again. Everything about Wembley was so impressive – the size, the style, the history, the importance. No wonder they called it 'The Home of Football'.

'It must be the best feeling ever to play on that pitch,' he thought to himself. 'Especially if you score!'

Jamie couldn't wait for the final to start, but it turned out to be a very long, rain-soaked night indeed. First, the kick-off was delayed by thirty minutes because many of the Wednesday fans were stuck in traffic on the motorway.

'Well, they should have just left Sheffield earlier,' his dad muttered under his breath next to him.

Then, when the game did eventually get started, it was a tight, tense battle between two well-matched teams. When Ian Wright gave Arsenal the lead in the first half, Jamie feared the worst, but Wednesday fought back strongly. John Harkes's cross flew just past Mark Bright's head, and then dropped down at Waddle's feet. He took the shot first time and it deflected up off an Arsenal defender and into the bottom corner. *1–1!*

As Waddle ran over to celebrate with the fans, Jamie was there, jumping for joy. 'Come on, Wednesday!' he screamed with passion. The crowd was still so loud that he couldn't even hear his own voice.

Both teams had brilliant chances to win the match, but in the last minute of extra time, the score was still 1–1. Although it was already well past his bedtime, Jamie was still wide awake, buzzing with nervous energy. Come on, Wednesday! But just as he was planning the penalty takers in his head, disaster struck. Paul Merson curled a corner into the box and up jumped Andrew Linighan to head the ball past Woods. *2–1!*

Wednesday were about to lose to Arsenal… again! Jamie couldn't bear it. The tears streamed down his cheeks and, just for a second, he even wished he'd gone to school instead. If only Brighty hadn't hit the post, if only Hirsty hadn't hit the side netting, if only Woodsy had saved Linighan's header… It was all so unfair! It was Jamie's first real experience of the deep pain of football defeat, and easily the worst feeling of his young life.

It was also, however, his first experience of the magic of Wembley and it stayed with him, despite the result. As he wiped his eyes that night and trudged out of the stadium, Jamie promised himself that he'd be back one day as a professional player, and that time, his team would win.

CHAPTER 5

WEDNESDAY WISH COME TRUE!

With dreams of Wembley in his head, Jamie couldn't wait to kick off his football career. He started going to training sessions at the local Hillsborough Leisure Centre and it didn't take long for the coaches to spot his talent.

'So, who d'you play for, kid?' they asked and then looked shocked to hear Jamie's answer:

'I don't have a team... yet.'

'What, a speedy striker like you?! We'll need to have a word with your parents about that...'

Soon, Jamie was starring for his first football club, York County, scoring goal after goal as if it was as easy as playing in the school playground. When he chased after a throughball, racing into the penalty area, there wasn't a single defender in the league who could catch him. And there wasn't a single keeper in the league who could save his powerful shots.

GOAL!

GOAL!

GOAL!

As much as Jamie loved that fantastic scoring feeling, it wasn't that much of a challenge for him. He was York County's best player by miles and after a couple of seasons, the games became a bit boring. It was clear to everyone who watched him that he was good enough to play at a higher level.

'I think it's time for you to test yourself,' Jamie's dad told him when he turned ten.

Luckily, one of Richard's fellow driving instructors, David Mace, was the manager of Sheffield Rangers. All the local kids had heard of Sheffield Rangers – they were one of the top local teams, who won game after game and trophy after trophy. Jamie certainly liked the sound of that! And after a couple of training sessions on trial, the deal was done. Jamie was joining Sheffield

Rangers as their speedy new striker.

'Just you watch,' he told his friends, 'I'm going to score more goals than ever!'

Although he knew that it would be a big step-up, Jamie always believed in his ability. He was a cheeky, confident kid, and nothing fazed him, not even a completely new environment. He was just going to keep doing what he did best and hopefully there would be scouts watching their games. After all, the manager's son, Daniel, was now playing at the Sheffield Wednesday academy.

That was Jamie's dream and it quickly came true. A year after joining Sheffield Rangers, his favourite football club offered him a trial at their training centre, Middlewood.

'Yes, I'm going to play for Wednesday!' he told everyone he saw.

It was the most amazing moment of Jamie's life, even better than going to Wembley. When the day of his first training session arrived at last, he felt a tiny bit nervous but mostly excited. He was following in the footsteps of Wednesday legends like Graham Hyde and Kevin Pressman, plus the 'next big things' like Lee Briscoe and Ritchie Humphreys.

'Let's do this!' Jamie told himself as he raced out onto the training pitch. He was determined to do everything possible to impress the academy coaches.

Jamie ran and ran, like an all-action football hero. He chased every ball and every defender, took every opportunity to shoot, and threw himself bravely into every tackle. Occasionally, his energy and aggression got him into a bit of trouble, but most of the time, it was a positive thing that helped his team to win.

'Honestly, he's a defender's worst nightmare!' one of the coaches said as they sat down to decide whether to offer Jamie a spot in their Under-12s squad.

'Yes, he's got determination, speed and a decent shot. But what about skill – is his technique good enough to play at the top level?'

'Well, there's only one way to find out!'

A few sessions later, Jamie heard the news he was hoping for – yes, Sheffield Wednesday wanted him to join their academy!

'Now, we'll just need you and your parents to read

through and sign the paperwork and then we can get your club kit sorted...'

But by then, Jamie had stopped listening and started celebrating. He had done it! All the way home and for the next few weeks, he felt on top of the world. He wanted everyone to know that his Wednesday wish had come true.

As a kid who loved football, Jamie was living out his fantasy. He was training with the Wednesday academy every Monday, Tuesday and Thursday, then watching the first team at Hillsborough on Saturdays (he had free tickets now!). And he was playing for the youth team on Sundays. What could possibly be better than that?

Even more football, that's what! Whenever he could, Jamie still turned up to play in the street matches with his mates. He loved having fun with his friends and even if he was on his way to becoming Wednesday's next star striker, he was still just one of the lads.

CHAPTER 6

A SPORTING STAR

'Woah, look,' one of Jamie's academy teammates
called out excitedly, pointing behind him. 'The first
team are here!'

At first, Jamie thought it was a joke to make him
turn around, but no, it was true. Sheffield Wednesday
didn't have a Premier League game that weekend,
so instead, the manager had brought his players to
Middlewood for an extra training session.

Woah, indeed! For a few minutes, Jamie stopped his
warm-up and just watched his heroes. Well, actually,
'stared' was more like it. He couldn't believe his eyes:
Pressman, Des Walker, Jim Magilton, and best of all,
the club's new Italian attackers, Benito Carbone and

Paolo Di Canio – they were all right there, just one football pitch away!

'Come on, concentrate!' Jamie's coach called out to him eventually. 'In case you've forgotten, we've got practice of our own to do.'

'Sorry!'

Jamie worked hard during all their training drills, but whenever he got a spare moment, he couldn't help sneaking a peek over at the next-door pitch. This was his chance to find out all the important information. What were the first team working on? Who was the fastest player? Who had the most powerful shot?

Even when their own session ended, Jamie stayed out on the pitch, kicking a ball around with one of the other academy players who was equally keen to spy on the senior squad. The two of them were still out there when their heroes wandered past.

'Hey, want a game?' they heard someone say in an Italian accent.

It was Di Canio, but who was he talking to? One of his teammates? No, when Jamie turned around,

Wednesday's star striker was looking straight at him. 'On my head, son!' he shouted with a smile.

Well, there was no way Jamie could say no to Di Canio! When he threw the ball up in the air, the Italian did a couple of headers and then flicked it on to Carbone, who controlled it perfectly and then carried on the skills show.

'Ok, let's a play a game – us versus you,' Di Canio decided after a few more headers. 'Ready?'

What?! A game of head tennis against Wednesday's two most skilful players?! Jamie and his teammate shared a terrified look, but what could they do? So, they said yes, knowing full well that they had no chance of winning.

While Jamie and his teammate just tried to get the ball over to the other side, Di Canio and Carbone were setting each other up for all kinds of tricks: neck rolls, back-heels, even bicycle kicks! It was incredible to watch, even if they couldn't compete.

'Good game, guys,' Di Canio said after a while, shaking hands with both of them before walking off with Carbone.

For a few moments, Jamie stood there, frozen still and speechless. Wow, had that really just happened? Yes, it had! It was an extra training session that neither he nor his teammate would ever forget.

Although Jamie clearly wasn't at Di Canio's level just yet, the signs were looking good for his future. His Wednesday dream was still alive, plus he was proving to be an all-round sporting star. He had the sprint speed to win the 100 metres and also the stamina to win the 1500 metres at his school's sports day. He was such a natural athlete, but as much as he enjoyed the medals and crossing the finish line first, nothing was as much fun as playing football. Sheffield Wednesday would always be his number one passion and focus. Always.

And so far, the club's academy director, Clive Baker, was very pleased with Jamie's progress. Each time he reached a new age group, he raised his game and kept scoring goals. On top of his phenomenal pace, the boy could shoot well with both feet, and he played with such bravery and passion. There wasn't a young defender in England who looked forward to facing

him. Maybe Jamie wasn't the most gifted footballer
at the academy, but his winning attitude and fighting
spirit would take him far. Yes, there was no reason
why he couldn't become Sheffield Wednesday's next
star striker, just as long as his growth spurt kicked in
soon…

CHAPTER 7

'NOT BIG ENOUGH'

As Jamie was rising up through the ranks at Sheffield Wednesday, his opponents were getting better and better. That didn't really faze him, because he enjoyed the challenge. He was good enough and brave enough to battle against any defender. Plus, he had a superpower of his own – his speed. Jamie backed himself to beat anyone in a race to a bouncing ball.

'Just give me something to chase and I'll score,' he promised his teammates, and he didn't let them down.

What did worry Jamie, however, was that his opponents were getting bigger and stronger. He, on the other hand, wasn't getting any taller.

'Why haven't I grown yet?' he grumbled almost every night at the dinner table to his mum and dad. 'Everyone else has!'

His parents urged him to be patient, but Jamie didn't feel he had time for that. He was playing for the Under-16s now, where size really mattered. He was going up against players like Tom Huddlestone at Derby County, who was already over six feet tall and powerful enough to play for the first team. Huddlestone towered over Jamie and outmuscled him too.

'What am I supposed to do?' Jamie shouted, throwing his skinny arms up in frustration. 'I've got no chance here!'

Jamie was spending more and more time on the Wednesday subs bench, now certain that his growth spurt would come eventually, and once it arrived, not even giants like Huddlestone would be able to stop him. He was sure of that. So, when his coaches called him in for a chat, Jamie didn't think there was anything to worry about. He thought he would just get the same good feedback as every other year, but he thought wrong.

'Thanks for coming in,' the coaches said as Jamie walked into the room and took a seat at the table. He didn't notice the worried looks on their faces until it was too late.

Times had changed at Sheffield Wednesday. Unfortunately, they were no longer the same trophy-chasing team they'd been in the 1990s. The golden era of Hirsty and Waddle was a thing of the past, and the days of Di Canio and Carbone were over too. Ten years after fighting for the Premier League title, they were now fighting relegation to the Second Division. The whole club was in crisis, from the first team all the way down to the youth team.

Yes, times had changed, and sadly so had the academy director. The new man in charge, Jimmy Shoulder, didn't share Clive Baker's faith in Jamie's bright future.

'Sorry kid, but we don't think you're big enough to make it as a striker.'

Jamie's jaw dropped, and so did his stomach. What, had he heard the man right – after five years at the academy, Wednesday were letting him go, just like that? Really, why now? Once the initial shock had worn off, those words kept repeating themselves in Jamie's head and each time they were like another sword through his broken heart.

'... *we don't think you're big enough to make it as a striker.*'

Jamie couldn't believe it. At the age of sixteen, his boyhood dream of playing for his local club, the club that he had supported all his young life, had just been crushed completely, with one shattering sentence. It was devastating, and there was nothing he could do about it because the decision had already been made. Becoming a professional footballer for his beloved Wednesday was all he had ever wanted, and he had been right on track to do it. But now, that was all over; now, his club didn't want him anymore. They had rejected him because they didn't think he was good enough. To Jamie, that was the worst news in the world; nothing else could compare to the hurt that was building up inside him.

The academy coaches were still talking, trying to

explain their decision, but Jamie wasn't listening. He was too angry and confused to take anything else in, or to ask the questions that were flying around his head:

What had he done wrong?

Why couldn't they wait a little longer for him to grow?

And what was he supposed to do now?

Suddenly, Jamie wished that he had studied harder at school. He had been so sure that he would be playing football for the Sheffield Wednesday first team when he was older that he hadn't even thought about a Plan B. But now it looked like that wasn't going to happen...

'If Wednesday don't want me, then I might as well give up on football altogether!' Jamie thought on his horrible journey home.

CHAPTER 8

STOCKSBRIDGE PARK STEELS

At first, Jamie felt totally lost without the club and the sport he loved – he didn't know what to do with all his new spare time, or where to go at the weekends. Mostly, he just stayed in, watching TV, and eating lots of unhealthy food.

But fortunately, Jamie didn't give up on football altogether. Once he'd had a few months to calm down and think, he changed his mind about that. Although it was going to take him a long time to get over his Sheffield Wednesday heartbreak, he still loved playing the game for fun. Instead of the harsh, competitive world of academy football, he wanted to go back to the good old days of kicking a ball around and having a laugh. So, when one of his friends from college invited him to go training with a local team, Jamie said yes.

'Why not? I can't keep sitting around at home, feeling sorry for myself!'

Wickersley Youth couldn't believe their luck when Jamie turned up, wanting to play. He got straight into their starting line-up and straight back to doing what he did best: sprinting past defenders and scoring lots of goals.

'Why on earth did Wednesday let him go?' his new teammates wondered. 'He's absolutely brilliant!' Jamie was good for Wickersley, and the team was good for him too. The players made him feel really welcome, and with each game and practice session, he could feel his confidence coming back, and his old passion for football returning.

Sadly for Wickersley, Jamie didn't stay at the club for long, though. One week, they played against the Stocksbridge Park Steels Under-18s and a certain speedy striker caught the manager's attention. With a bit of detective work, Steve Adams got Jamie's mobile phone number and gave him a call.

'I want you to come and play for us,' he tried to persuade him.

Stocksbridge Park Steels weren't exactly Sheffield Wednesday; they played in the Northern Premier League Division One South, which was seven tiers below the Premier League. But as Adams showed Jamie when he went along to watch training, the club had good facilities and a proper, professional set-up – youth teams and Reserves, as well as the first team.

'You'd be starting off in the Under-18s,' Adams said, 'but if you keep playing like you did against us at the weekend, you won't be there for long!'

Why not? Jamie decided to give it a go. It sounded like the perfect next step. At Stocksbridge, he would get to play at a decent level, but without the pressures of being at a top club. He would be able to relax and enjoy his football.

Life at Stocksbridge wasn't quite that straightforward, however. The club's home ground, Bracken Moor, was at the top of a hill, and as Jamie soon discovered, there was no protection from the weather. Learning to cope with the lashing rain, howling winds and layers of snow was all part of the challenge of playing for Stocksbridge.

Challenge accepted! Jamie stayed in the Under-18s for two seasons in the end, building up his fitness and confidence again. There was no rush to reach the first team; he was enjoying himself and that was the main thing. His painful experience at Wednesday was in the past, and so was his dream of playing professionally. Now, football was just about having fun with friends. Jamie felt settled at Stocksbridge and he was scoring almost every game. Even when the winter weather was against him, he could still beat any defender to the ball and shoot past any keeper.

'Nice one, J!' his teammates cried out as they celebrated another goal together.

So, ahead of Jamie's third season at the club, Adams decided that his speedy young striker was ready to test himself at a higher level. Suddenly, his weekends were football-filled again: Reserves match on Saturday, then Under-18s on Sunday.

There were no complaints from Jamie; he couldn't

wait to compete against proper, powerful adults. And fortunately, his growth spurt had arrived at last, less than six months after Sheffield Wednesday had told him he wasn't big enough. Typical! So, although Jamie was still skinny, at least he wasn't small for his age anymore. And, of course, he wasn't scared of anything or anyone.

'Bring it on!' Jamie told his new teammates confidently.

It took him a few games, but he soon found his scoring touch for the Reserves too. The Stocksbridge midfielders knew all about Jamie's speed and so they tried to slip the ball through to him whenever they could. As they launched another hopeful pass over the top, *ZOOM!* Jamie burst past the opposition defence, got to the ball first, and then dribbled into the box. The keeper decided to rush out and dive at his feet, so Jamie just lifted the ball over him with a cheeky chip.

Goooooooooooooooooooooaaaaaaaaaaaaaaaaalllllllllllllllll llllllllllllll!!!!!!!!!!!!!!!!!!!

Jamie jogged over towards the corner flag and then slid across the mud on his knees. He loved football again, and most of all, he loved scoring. There was no greater feeling in the world.

And not only was Jamie hitting the back of the net on a regular basis for the Stocksbridge Reserves, with his energy and aggression he was causing all kinds of problems for defenders, too. Every time his team went forward on the attack, he was off, sprinting towards the goal like it was an Olympic 100m race. And every time his team lost possession, he chased around the pitch tirelessly until he won it back.

'I'm so glad you're on our team,' one of the Stocksbridge centre-backs told Jamie after another all-action performance up front. 'Even in training, you're a nightmare to play against, so it must be awful in an actual match!'

CHAPTER 9

FROM FOOTBALL TO THE FACTORY

Playing for Stocksbridge Park Steels, Jamie had found his passion for football again. His love for the beautiful game was back and as strong as ever. He looked forward to every training session and every match. There was only one problem – money.

Stocksbridge was a fun, pressure-free environment for a young footballer, but Jamie was playing for free, at least until he reached the first team. And even then, he wouldn't get paid very much; nothing compared to the wages at Sheffield Wednesday or one of the clubs in the Premier League.

But Jamie didn't have the desire to dream big again. He had tried that, and it hadn't worked out well. He was happy at Stocksbridge, so instead he looked for jobs that he could do alongside his football. First, Jamie tried working in a bar, but the manager at Stocksbridge wanted him to train or play at the weekends, so that wasn't going to work! Next, he got a job as a joiner, building furniture for people's houses, but the long hours and tiring work left him exhausted.

'I've barely got enough energy to get out of bed,' he complained to his teammates, 'let alone race around a football field for ninety minutes!'

In the end, Jamie moved on and got a new job in a local factory that made medical products. Although it was hard, heavy work, he got on really well with his colleagues and the bosses were understanding about his football career. If Jamie needed to take a few hours off one afternoon to get to a midweek game, then that was no problem.

'Good luck – go and score a goal or two!' they told him, and he didn't disappoint.

In fact, by the time the 2007–08 season kicked off, Jamie's sharpshooting had finally earned him a call-up to the Stocksbridge first team squad, at the age of twenty. During preseason training, their new manager, Gary Marrow, spotted that he had something special and offered him an opportunity to prove it.

Jamie jumped at the chance and he made the most of it, even though it meant sometimes playing out of position on the wing. Whatever the manager asked him to do, Jamie did it, with 100 per cent effort and 0 per cent fear. The big non-league defenders didn't expect Stocksbridge's skinny new striker to be so brave, aggressive, and difficult to play against. And his speed and shooting ability meant that there was little they could do to stop him.

Goooooooooooooooooooaaaaaaaaaaaaaaaalllllllllllllll llllllllllll!!!!!!!!!!!!!!!!!!

Goooooooooooooooooooaaaaaaaaaaaaaaaalllllllllllllll llllllllllll!!!!!!!!!!!!!!!!!!

By the end of his first season, Jamie had become a regular starter and scorer, as well as a big, confident character in the dressing room. There was a strong team spirit at the club, and once he had settled in, Jamie was never shy to get involved in the banter. The pranks, the nicknames, the funny goal celebrations, the drinks after the games – that was all an important part of football for him, and key to building a happy, successful football team.

And that's what Stocksbridge had become by the time the 2008–09 season started. Thanks to the bond between the players, both on and off the pitch, the team was now unbeatable. They scored goal after goal, winning game after game. It turned out to be an unforgettable year for Jamie and his friends. First, they won the final of the Sheffield and Hallamshire Senior Cup at Wednesday's Hillsborough Stadium and then they beat Belper Town in the playoff final to earn promotion to the premier division of the Northern Premier League, for the first time in the club's history. What a team, and what an achievement!

Jamie felt really proud to be a part of it, and with over twenty goals that season, he was pleased with his own progress too. He had worked so hard for his team and proved his quality on the pitch. Now, it was time to relax and get the promotion party started. He was at the centre of the club celebrations, spraying champagne all over everyone. Although he was shirtless, he was wearing a blue-and-yellow Stocksbridge flag like a superhero cape and the lid of the trophy as a hat.

'You're one of a kind, you are Vards!' his teammates laughed when they saw his new look.

'I think that's probably for the best, really!' they all agreed afterwards.

But despite his success on the football field, there was no chance of Jamie getting carried away. Because after being Stocksbridge's star striker on a Sunday afternoon, he was back at work in the factory by the Monday morning.

CHAPTER 10

THE ELLA EFFECT

At the age of twenty-two, Jamie's sole aim in life was to enjoy every moment. He had a laugh working at the factory and a laugh playing football with his friends at the weekend. What could be better than that? He had moved on from his Sheffield Wednesday heartbreak, and now he had no real ambition to play professionally anymore. He was happy to stay at Stocksbridge, where they didn't take things too seriously. Jamie's life suited him perfectly. He never let his team down on the pitch, but at the same time, he never missed a wild night out with his mates. As long as he didn't have a match the next day, he was free to do whatever he wanted – to eat as much fast food as he liked, and to go out partying whenever he pleased.

But that all changed in April 2010, when Jamie's first daughter was born. Yes, Ella's arrival changed everything because suddenly, it wasn't all about him anymore. Jamie had a child to take care of now; he had to step up and take responsibility. For the first time in ages, he needed to think about the future. Could he really support a child with his combined wages from football and his work at the factory?

Although he loved his life at Stocksbridge, Jamie was sure that with a bit more focus and discipline, he could definitely play for a bigger team, where he would earn more money. He had serious potential as a footballer, as he had proved away at FC United of Manchester earlier that season. Picking up the ball well within his own half, Jamie had sprinted forward on a solo dribble. There wasn't a teammate in sight and when three defenders chased him back into position, it looked like Jamie was surrounded, and the opportunity had been wasted. But no, all of a sudden he glided between two United players, then past another, as he turned on his turbo speed boost.

ZOOM! He was into the penalty area now, where the keeper was rushing out towards him. So, with a calm left foot finish, Jamie rolled the ball past him and into the bottom corner.

Goooooooooooooooooooaaaaaaaaaaaaaaaaalllllllllllllll llllllllllll!!!!!!!!!!!!!!!!!!!

'What a good goal from the Stocksbridge Number 11!' cried the commentator on the video highlights.

It was a clip that Jamie watched again and again, and he wasn't the only one. Scouts had been watching him for years, and he had even had trials at a couple of clubs in the Football League, Crewe Alexandra and Rotherham United. Back then, Jamie hadn't shown much interest in joining another football club, but that was before he became a father. Now, he was determined to impress the scouts by scoring more goals than ever. Oh, and by not getting sent off so often...

Ella turned out to be the extra motivation Jamie needed to knuckle down and make the jump. Despite a few injuries, he still finished the season as one of Stocksbridge's top scorers. Right, so were there any bigger teams that wanted to sign him?

Although FC Halifax Town were in the same division as Stocksbridge, the Northern Premier League Premier Division, they weren't planning on staying there for long. Once upon a time, the club had been in League Two, but due to money problems, they'd had to start again from the bottom. Now, they were aiming to get back up to the Football League as quickly as possible and so they needed a new goalscorer to fire them there.

After talking to the manager, Neil Aspin, Jamie was happy to move to Halifax. He could tell that it was a bigger club, with a lot more ambition, and a lot more money too. They agreed to pay £15,000 to sign him, which was a lot for non-league football, and they also doubled his wages.

'Happy days!' Jamie thought to himself as he signed his new contract. Although it would be sad saying goodbye to all of his friends at Stocksbridge, this was an offer he just couldn't refuse. His old teammates would understand that it was time for him to think about his future, and of course, his daughter Ella.

Most people thought that Halifax were taking a big risk, especially on a player who had been sent off four times in one season. But not their manager; Aspin wasn't worried about Jamie's bad-boy reputation. All he saw was a striker with super speed, a wonderful work-rate, and a great goalscoring record.

'The guy's got everything we need,' he assured his club chairman.

And Aspin was right. On the opening day of the 2010–11 campaign, Halifax beat Buxton 2–1 at home at The Shay. And who scored the winner? Jamie, of course! Collecting a long ball from the back, he dribbled into the box and, before any defenders could stop him, he blasted a powerful shot past the keeper.

Goooooooooooooooooooooaaaaaaaaaaaaaaaaalllllllllllllll llllllllllll!!!!!!!!!!!!!!!!!!

As he raced away to celebrate, Jamie raised one arm up in the air, just like the top Premier League striker, Alan Shearer. Yes, Halifax's new Number 10 was already feeling super-confident about the season ahead.

CHAPTER 11

HAT-TRICKS AT HALIFAX

It took a few weeks, but Halifax soon hit top form, thanks to their super new strike partnership. Jamie and Danny Holland clicked straight away, and they turned out to be a very dangerous duo, both on the football field and in the dressing room. They were always laughing and planning new pranks to play on the other players. Their manager didn't mind a bit of banter, as long as his team kept winning…

Halifax 5 Whitby 1,
Halifax 4 Hucknall 0,
Marine 0 Halifax 6!

Playing alongside Danny, Jamie was looking more lethal than ever. He was using his smart football brain, as well as his speed. When a Marine defender slipped, Vardy pounced in a flash and fired a shot past the keeper. A few minutes later, he made a clever late run to convert a cross from the wing. *GOAL! GOAL!* Jamie was scoring so often that sometimes he didn't even get excited anymore. Hat-tricks, however, were different – they were definitely worth celebrating.

With ten minutes to go, Halifax were heading for a 1–0 defeat at home against Chasetown. Jamie was furious; his team's performance was nowhere near good enough and they were running out of time to turn things around. But as a defender delivered a long ball into the Chasetown box, Danny won the flick-on and it found its way through to Jamie. He had sneaked in unmarked at the back post and he wasn't going to miss from six yards out. *1–1!*

'Come on!' he cried out passionately as his teammates hugged him. 'Let's go and win this now!'

Five minutes later, Jamie was on the run, chasing after another long ball from the back. He reached it just before the defender, who tried but failed to muscle him out of the way. 'No chance!' Jamie said, shrugging him off, before calmly chesting the ball down and then lobbing it over the keeper's head. His shot looked like it was going in, but he gave it another big kick just to make sure. *2–1!*

'Yessssssssss!' Jamie yelled as he stood in front of the Halifax supporters with both arms up. He even did a little celebration dance with Danny.

But the match wasn't over yet. Chasetown managed to equalise in injury time, leaving Halifax with seconds left to score a winner. Luckily for them, Jamie was on a roll and on a hat-trick. Their keeper kicked it long to Danny, who flicked it on to his strike partner once again. Jamie was on the edge of the penalty area, with his back to goal and a defender right behind him, but with three quick touches, he spun into the space and got his shot away. *BANG!* The ball flew like a rocket into the top corner of the net.

Goooooooooooooooooooooaaaaaaaaaaaaaaaaallllllllllllllll llllllllllll!!!!!!!!!!!!!!!!!!!!

He had done it; Jamie was Halifax's hat-trick hero! With the buzz rushing through his body, he sprinted towards the corner flag and then slid across the grass.

When he got back up, Jamie blew kisses to the roaring crowd, who were chanting his name loudly and proudly. What a phenomenal feeling!

A week later, Jamie was at it again, away at Kendal Town. With a brave header and then two left-foot strikes, he helped Halifax to a 4–2 win and made it back-to-back hat-tricks. To celebrate his special achievement, Jamie cheekily pulled down his shorts to show off his lucky red pants!

'Mate, I know you're doing well at the moment, but we don't need to see that!' Danny laughed.

Jamie was on fire and he felt unstoppable. He was scoring with almost every shot, so a hat-trick of hat-tricks? Why not?!

He got off to a great start against Nantwich Town with a clever, glancing header into the bottom corner. Then in the second half, Jamie made it two with one of his trademark runs. Chasing onto a through-ball, he sprinted past the last defender and then smashed it past the keeper.

Goooooooooooooooooooooaaaaaaaaaaaaaaaaallllllllllllll llllllllllll!!!!!!!!!!!!!!!!!!!

It was a brilliant move, but he made it look so easy. Jamie jogged over to the Halifax supporters behind the goal and just stood there in front of them, arms out, enjoying every moment. Eight goals in three games – it was a remarkable record, but he was still hungry for one more...

Sadly, despite all his energy and desire, Jamie couldn't quite complete his third consecutive hat-trick. But he wasn't too disappointed about that because he soon had more important things to think about, like snaring the Northern Premier League Premier Division title. Halifax finished a whopping nineteen points clear at the top of the table.

'We are going up! Say, we are going up!' Jamie chanted along with all of his teammates.

It was a very proud moment for him, and this time, the promotion celebrations weren't quite as wild as they'd been two seasons earlier at Stocksbridge. At the end of Halifax's final home game versus Mickleover Sports, the players climbed the steep steps up to the top of the stand to lift the league title in front of all the fans. Then, it was back down onto the pitch for lots of photos and plenty more singing.

Campeones, Campeones, Olé! Olé! Olé!

Barmy Army, Barmy Army, Barmy Army!

There's only one Jamie Vardy, one Jamie Vardy!

What a season it had been, both for the club and for their double hat-trick hero. The risky move to sign Jamie had really paid off and he was now ready to play at a higher level. With twenty-four goals, he was one of the top scorers in the league, as well as one of the most talked-about strikers around. Halifax would be playing in the Conference North (now called The National League North) next season, but would Jamie be joining them? Or was he destined for bigger and better things?

CHAPTER 12

FLYING HIGHER AT FLEETWOOD

Step by step and hat-trick by hat-trick, Jamie was climbing his way up England's long football ladder, but he still wasn't taking things too seriously. When a club reporter asked him if he'd be staying at Halifax next season, he jokingly replied, 'No, I'm signing for Ibiza Town. I'm going there on holiday and I'm never coming back!'

Jamie was just living in the moment, seeing how far his football adventures would take him. He didn't really think about any bigger ambitions – until the day he met John Morris. Morris was a football agent for a company that looked after lots of top professional players, including England international,

Theo Walcott. So, what was he doing talking to an unknown, non-league footballer like Jamie? Well, as it happened, Morris knew the Halifax goalkeeper, who had told him about his team's new and speedy star striker, who was scoring goals for fun. At first, Morris wasn't that interested in this, but after seeing Jamie Vardy in action, he changed his mind completely.

'You've got everything,' he told Jamie enthusiastically when he agreed to meet him. 'You can do whatever you want in this game. You can go on and play for England–'

When he heard that, Jamie couldn't help laughing, but Morris continued. 'Really. That's how good you are.'

Jamie knew that football agents weren't always the most reliable people, but there was something about the way Morris spoke to him that made him trust the man. Besides, it was worth a go, wasn't it? Jamie was twenty-four now, and so his chances of ever playing professional football were getting slimmer and slimmer all the time. That meant Morris's offer was one he couldn't refuse, so Jamie said yes and signed up to be his latest client.

'So, who wants to buy me then?' he asked his new agent, getting straight down to business.

Although Jamie's hat-tricks had attracted a lot of attention, there was a problem – money. Halifax had set his transfer fee at £150,000, which was a lot to pay for a striker who had never even played in the Football League. Would any clubs be willing to buy him for that much?

As Jamie waited, hoping to hear good news from Morris, he made a big, bold choice. After four years of working at the factory, he decided to wave goodbye to it. He would miss his colleagues, but not the hard, sweaty work. And although it was a financial risk, he wanted to focus on his football, even if he did end up staying at Halifax for another year... But just when Jamie had given up hope, a deal was done. He was on his way to Fleetwood Town!

Fleetwood were playing in the Conference Premier, which was one league higher than Halifax. However, their chairman, Andy Pilley, had big plans to take the club into the Football League as quickly as possible, and he didn't mind spending money to get there.

'Fleetwood are a team on the up and I want to be part of that,' Jamie told journalists as he arrived at his new club.

There was no time to chat and settle in, however. The new league season was already underway, so on the same day he signed, Jamie went straight into the Fleetwood starting line-up against York City. The match finished 0–0, but he was pleased with his first performance and so was his new manager, Micky Mellon.

'With your speed and energy, the defenders in this league are going to really hate playing against you!' he said with a smile.

Playing for Fleetwood really felt like a step-up. Although they were still a non-league team, the set-up was very professional. Suddenly, Jamie had training sessions every day and his name on the back of his shirt, as well as his number – '33 VARDY'.

'Lads, I've finally made it big!' he joked with his mates.

Football was starting to get serious for Jamie.

Now that he wasn't working in the factory, he had more energy and felt a lot fresher, and now that he was training every day, he felt a lot sharper on his game, too. Soon enough, he was showing these improvements on the pitch for Fleetwood.

Jamie looked like he was about to run the ball out of play, but instead, he slid the ball into the net from an impossible angle... *GOAL!*

Racing onto a teammate's pass, he didn't even take a touch before calmly lifting the ball over the diving keeper...

GOAL!

'There is nothing more certain than Jamie Vardy scoring when he sets his eye on the net!'

He made it all look so easy. Jamie had the speed to outsprint anyone, the smart football brain to make the right runs at the right time, and the shooting accuracy to hit the back of the net from any angle and any distance...

GOAL!

Each season, Jamie was testing himself at a higher level, against better teams and better defenders, and he was consistently coming out on top, scoring goal after goal after goal. In fact, the better his opponents, the better he became. In the FA Cup, Fleetwood defeated two League One clubs, and Jamie scored in both games.

In the First Round, he hit Wycombe Wanderers on the counter-attack with a cool, left-foot finish.

Goooooooooooooooooooooaaaaaaaaaaaaaaaalllllllllllllll llllllllllllll!!!!!!!!!!!!!!!!!!!!

Jamie slid across the grass on his knees and then stood there, pointing to the back of his shirt. 'VARDY' – it was a name that the celebrating Fleetwood fans would never forget.

Neither would the Yeovil Town defenders, who he terrorised in the Second Round. First, Bondz N'Gala was sent off for fouling Jamie twice, and then later on, Paul Huntington found himself one on one with Fleetwood's star striker. As Jamie dribbled forward, the centre-back tried his best to stop him cutting inside and shooting with his right foot, but what he didn't know was that Jamie was just as good with his left foot. *BANG!*

Goooooooooooooooooooooaaaaaaaaaaaaaaaaalllllllllllllll llllllllllllll!!!!!!!!!!!!!!!!!!!!!

It was already Jamie's fifteenth goal of the season, and it was still only December! Would Blackpool be able to stop Fleetwood's danger man in the FA Cup Third Round? No, even though his team lost 5–1, Jamie still got his name on the scoresheet. Pouncing on a sloppy pass, he burst between two defenders and then slotted the ball into the bottom corner with style.

Goooooooooooooooooooooaaaaaaaaaaaaaaaaalllllllllllllll llllllllllllll!!!!!!!!!!!!!!!!!!!!!

Jamie had passed yet another tough test; not even a Championship team could keep Fleetwood's top scorer quiet. It looked like his agent, Morris, was right about his amazing ability after all; there were certainly a lot of clubs paying attention to him now.

Finally, at the age of twenty-five, was Jamie Vardy good enough to start playing professional football?

CHAPTER 13

A £1-MILLION MAN

Blackpool were the first team to try to buy Jamie during the January transfer window. 'What a wonderful player!' their manager, Ian Holloway, told the media after their FA Cup tie. But Fleetwood stood firm and wouldn't budge – their star striker was worth £1 million, and not a penny less.

A million pounds? Jamie couldn't believe it. Surely, that was far too high a price for a non-league player? But no, there were clubs who were willing to spend that much money, including Championship clubs Leicester City and Southampton. That was the good news. The bad news was that the Fleetwood chairman refused to let him leave just yet.

'Look, I didn't pay £150,000 for only five months of football,' Pilley explained. 'If we keep this form going, we could be playing in League Two next season. Stay and help us get there. You can go wherever you like after that. But you've got to get the job done first.'

Sadly, Jamie's professional football career would have to wait a little longer. He wasn't happy about it, but there was nothing he could do, except focus on finishing off what he'd started at Fleetwood by helping to get them promoted...

Fleetwood Town 3 Braintree Town 1 – one more goal for Jamie,

AFC Telford 1 Fleetwood Town 4 – two more goals for Jamie,

Fleetwood Town 6 Ebbsfleet United 2 – three more goals for Jamie!

It was a great feeling to be a hat-trick hero once again, and this was one that Jamie would never forget because his goals got better and better as the game went on.

The first was a simple tap-in, a rebound after the keeper had saved Magno Vieira's long-range strike.

'Nice one, Vards!' Gareth Seddon cheered, giving his teammate a high-five.

But Jamie was only just getting started. Early in the second half, he dribbled in off the right wing, speeding past the Ebbsfleet defender in a flash, before firing a perfect finish into the bottom corner with the outside of his right foot.

Goooooooooooooooooooaaaaaaaaaaaaaaaallllllllllllll llllllllllll!!!!!!!!!!!!!!!!!!

Jamie jogged slowly over to the corner flag as if it was no big deal, but the huge grin on his face told the truth. He was delighted to score such a high-quality goal. What a clever run, and what a classy finish! It was proof for all the scouts watching that he had plenty of skill as well as pace.

And there was more proof to come because Jamie had saved his best until last. Ten minutes later, he ran forward with the ball, over the halfway line, and as the defenders backed away, he had the time and space to look up.

'Shoot!' he heard his Fleetwood teammate Lee Fowler shout from midfield.

Really? Jamie was about fifty yards from goal and the Ebbsfleet keeper wasn't even that far off his line. There was only a tiny chance of scoring, but why not? He had the cheeky confidence to give it a go. *BANG!*

Jamie could tell straight away that he'd struck the ball sweetly and he stood and watched as it flew towards the target. It was either going to be a comfortable catch for the keeper, or Jamie's shot would sail just over his up-stretched arms... When he saw that the ball was dropping just under his crossbar, the keeper panicked, back-pedalling as quickly as he could. Although he did get a glove on Jamie's shot, he couldn't stop it from crossing the line.

Goooooooooooooooooooooooaaaaaaaaaaaaaaaalllllllllllllll llllllllllll!!!!!!!!!!!!!!!!!!!

What a way to complete his hat-trick! Even Jamie looked a little surprised by his wonderstrike, as his teammates surrounded him, giving him hugs and slaps on the back.

'That's too good, mate,' Lee said, shaking his head in amazement. 'Too good.'

It wasn't just Jamie, though; as a whole team,

Fleetwood were too good for the Conference Premier. They hadn't lost a league game since October! 'The Trawlermen' had so much attacking talent in their squad that Mellon sometimes played with four strikers at the same time. The result was goals galore! So, it was no surprise that in mid-April, Fleetwood were crowned Champions with two games to spare. Job done! It was another year, another league title for Jamie.

Campeones, Campeones, Olé! Olé! Olé!

'I'm getting used to lifting trophies!' he joked as the team danced around the dressing room in delight. Just like during the old days at Stocksbridge, Jamie was at the centre of the celebrations, shirtless and spraying champagne everywhere.

Then one by one, the Fleetwood players walked back out onto the pitch to a hero's welcome from the crowd. And who got the biggest cheer? Jamie, of course! Of Fleetwood's phenomenal 102 league goals, Jamie had grabbed thirty-one of them, in only thirty-six games.

So, what next for the Conference Premier's top

scorer? Jamie had really enjoyed his first season at Fleetwood. It was so much fun playing up front for a team that created chance after chance. But while his teammates were looking forward to playing in League Two, Jamie was hoping to be playing at an even higher level.

'Right, which Championship clubs still want me?' he asked his agent once the season was over.

There were three teams leading the race to sign Fleetwood's £1-million man: Peterborough United, Cardiff City, and Leicester City. Jamie had meetings with all three managers, but it didn't take him long to make up his mind:

LEICESTER CITY

There were lots of good reasons for going there: Leicester was the closest to Sheffield, the club had been chasing him for years, they had an amazing stadium and training facilities, and they were managed by one of Jamie's childhood heroes, Sheffield Wednesday's Nigel Pearson.

'This year, our target is promotion to the Premier League,' Pearson told Jamie, after inviting him to his house, 'and we want you to be a big part of that.'

That sounded absolutely brilliant, but just in case he still wasn't convinced, Leicester even offered Jamie the Number 9 shirt. 'Done!' he told Morris with an eager smile. 'Where do I sign?'

A few days later, Jamie was posing for photos in the stands at the King Power Stadium, holding a blue club scarf high above his head. As well as being Leicester City's latest signing, he was also the most expensive non-league player of all time.

'So, how does it feel?' friends and family kept asking him.

It felt like a fairytale, too good to be true, and yet, this life-changing moment was really happening. Three years earlier he had been playing for Stocksbridge Park Steels, but now Jamie was about to become a Championship player. He would be starring in the same Leicester team as Kasper Schmeichel, Paul Konchesky, Jermaine Beckford and David Nugent – top players he'd admired from afar. Plus, Vardy was now just one league away from achieving his childhood dream of playing in the Premier League!

As crazy as the situation was, however, Jamie managed to stay calm, confident, and focused. 'I believe in my own ability,' he told the local newspaper. 'And, hopefully, the goals will be coming thick and fast.'

CHAPTER 14

TOUGH TIMES AT LEICESTER CITY

During his early days at Leicester, Jamie felt a bit of an outsider. The new guy in a very talented team. Did he really fit in amongst such amazing footballers? With each preseason practice, however, the club felt a little more like home. It helped that Jamie got on really well with the other players, especially his fellow striker, David Nugent. 'Nuge' had spent several seasons in the Premier League, with Portsmouth and Burnley, and he had even played for England.

'One cap, one goal,' he told Jamie with a mix of pride and humour. 'Not many players have a 100 per cent scoring record at international level!'

'Yeah, I remember watching that game,' Jamie

replied straight away. 'Didn't you steal Jermain Defoe's goal by kicking it over the line?'

'I don't know what you're talking about,' 'Nuge' said with a wink and a smile. 'A defender was coming in to clear it, so I had to make sure!'

The laughter and jokes helped Jamie settle into the Leicester squad, and by the time the new season started in August 2012, he had done enough to impress his new manager too. After scoring on his club debut in the League Cup against Torquay United, Pearson put him straight into the starting line-up for their opening Championship clash with Peterborough.

New league, no problem! On his league debut, Jamie set up Leicester's second goal in a 2–0 win, and then a week later, he scored his first for his new club. Away at Blackburn, he pounced on a poor backpass and raced in to beat the keeper to the ball. Then, in front of 14,000 spectators, Jamie showed real composure to slide a shot into the bottom corner.

Goooooooooooooooooooooaaaaaaaaaaaaaaaaaalllllllllllllll llllllllllllll!!!!!!!!!!!!!!!!!!!

Yes, he was off the mark in the Championship! As

he raced over to the Leicester fans, Jamie leapt up and punched the air. He felt on top of the world, like he could achieve anything.

'No need to thank me for the assist,' his strike partner said as they celebrated the goal together.

Jamie just laughed. 'You didn't even touch the ball, Nuge. You can't fool me; I saw it flick off the defender's head instead!'

After two more strikes against Burnley and Middlesbrough, Jamie was feeling good about life at Leicester City. He was pretty happy with three goals and three assists in his first ten matches. No, he wasn't scoring as often as he had at his other clubs yet, but that was understandable. The Championship was full of top defenders, with pace as well as power. It would just take time for him to find his old Fleetwood form...

Unfortunately, after a promising start, Jamie stopped scoring and that was a big problem for the team. It wouldn't have mattered so much if Leicester were still winning, but they weren't; suddenly, they were either losing or drawing most weeks. Why? The answer was simple and obvious – they weren't scoring enough goals. Without a sharpshooting striker, 'The Foxes' slipped from top of the table to second, then fourth, then fifth...

Uh-oh, Leicester's promotion to the Premier League was in real danger. As the games went by and Jamie couldn't grab any more goals, the manager had no choice but to make a change. Pearson decided to put Martyn Waghorn up front with Nuge instead. At first, Jamie dropped down to the bench, but his performances didn't get any better as a super sub, and so he was left out of Leicester's matchday squad altogether.

Pearson could see his player's disappointment. 'Sorry, son. You'll be back playing again soon, I promise.'

But Jamie wasn't so sure about that. It felt like his big professional football adventure had gone badly wrong already. Was the Championship a step too far? Maybe he just wasn't good enough, after all. Even when he came on for sixty minutes during his team's 6–0 thrashing of Ipswich Town, he still couldn't score.

'Noooooo!' Jamie groaned, kicking the air in frustration. He could hear what the 20,000 fans thought of him and it was all over social media too.

'One million pounds? What a waste of money that was!'

Jamie's smile was gone, and so was his confidence. For the first time in years, he wasn't enjoying his football at all, and his focus had slipped. Instead of working harder in practice to get back to his best, Jamie was going out with his mates to try and escape from his troubles. His sleeping pattern was all over the place, and his diet was dreadful. Although he was a professional footballer now, he certainly wasn't acting like one.

'Everything okay, J?' Nuge asked as he watched his teammate trudge his way through training, but Jamie just nodded his head and carried on. He didn't want to talk about it.

Then to make matters even worse, in January 2013, Jamie slipped further down the list of Leicester attackers. The club signed Chris Wood from West Brom and also brought in a young Tottenham forward on loan: Harry Kane.

Well, now they definitely didn't need a struggling striker like Jamie. Was it time for a fresh start somewhere else? After thinking long and hard, he decided to go and speak to his manager about going back to Fleetwood on loan for the rest of the season, just to find his scoring form again.

Pearson, however, said no straight away. He looked Jamie in the eyes and told him, 'You're not going anywhere, lad. You're good enough to succeed at this football club.'

It was nice to hear such positivity from his manager, and Jamie would just have to be patient and wait for his opportunity to play again. For the rest of the season, he stayed stuck on the bench, watching Leicester squeeze their way into the Championship play-offs without him. When they lost to Watford in the semi-finals, there was nothing Jamie could do to help.

'Unlucky, lads,' he told his teammates as he walked around the pitch after the final whistle.

Jamie was disappointed that Leicester wouldn't be going up to the Premier League, but at the same time, he felt some relief, because finally it was the end of his first season to forget. Five goals in twenty-nine games – those numbers were nowhere near good enough. But after a relaxing summer holiday, Jamie would be back to try again: new season, new start.

CHAPTER 15

PROMOTION TO THE PREMIER LEAGUE

Yes, Jamie was determined to turn things around at Leicester City. Even on his summer holiday, he went out running every day to work on his fitness. With his manager's support, he was going to prove people wrong and become a top Championship striker. The 2013–14 season was all set to be his greatest yet.

When the players returned for preseason training, Nuge noticed the difference straight away. 'Woah, what's got into you, J? You've got a spring in your step again!'

Pearson soon spotted Jamie's progress too. So, for the first game of the new Championship season, he put him back into the starting line-up, and he didn't disappoint. Midway through the second half, Leicester broke away on the counter-attack. Jamie flicked a header onto Nuge, who slipped the ball through for the one-two. ZOOM! Jamie's first touch was a heavy one, but fortunately he had the super-speed to get there just before the Middlesbrough centre-back. This was a chance he wasn't going to miss. With his right foot, he curled the ball into the top corner. *2–1 to Leicester!*

Goooooooooooooooooooaaaaaaaaaaaaaaaallllllllllllll llllllllllll!!!!!!!!!!!!!!!!!!!!

As Jamie jogged over to the corner flag to celebrate, he tried to escape from Nuge's grip, but his strike partner wasn't letting go.

'Yes, you hero!' he yelled in Jamie's ear.

That goal turned out to be the matchwinner, and it gave Jamie the confidence boost he needed. His self-belief was back. He could do this; he could fire Leicester City into the Premier League.

At first, Jamie wasn't scoring every week, but his team was winning, and he was playing a big part. His shot led to an own goal against Derby County and he used his pace to win penalties against Wigan Athletic and Barnsley.

'Nice one, J!' Nuge said after scoring from the spot.

And as the season went on, Jamie found his own top scoring form again. He grabbed back-to-back goals against Huddersfield Town and Bournemouth, and then got two more against Millwall. The great news for Leicester was that both were classic Jamie strikes. For the first, he dribbled the ball all the way from the halfway line to the penalty area, before nutmegging the keeper. And for the second, he raced in to pounce on a bad backpass.

Goooooooooooooooooooaaaaaaaaaaaaaaaalllllllllllll llllllllllll!!!!!!!!!!!!!!!!!!

'Get in!' Nuge cheered as he jumped on Jamie's back. Finally, they were forming the perfect strike partnership, with fifteen goals between them by the start of December.

That win against Millwall moved Leicester to the top of the Championship table. So, could they stay there until the end of the season? Things didn't look good after two defeats in a row, but their strikers saved them. Nuge scored a penalty to earn a point against Burnley, and then Jamie got the winner away at QPR. As 2014 began, The Foxes were back at the top of the league.

'Now, we need to stay there!' Pearson urged his players.

A few weeks later, Jamie scored his tenth goal of the season to give Leicester a late victory away at Birmingham City. What a feeling! He had doubled his 2012–13 goal total already, and he hadn't even hit top form yet. That came during the second half of the season, after some lessons from a Premier League legend. Former Sunderland and Southampton striker Kevin Phillips joined Leicester in January, and he took Jamie under his wing straight away. After training, they worked together on what runs he should make and how he should finish in different situations. Jamie felt so lucky to be learning from one of the best in the business.

'Once you're in the box, you've got to slow things down,' Kevin told him. 'There's no need to smash it as hard as you can every time! Think about where you want your shot to go and then guide the ball there.'

When Jamie put his teammate's advice into practice on the pitch, suddenly he couldn't stop scoring, against:

Nottingham Forest,

Ipswich,

Charlton,

Barnsley,

Blackburn.

They were all important goals too, helping Leicester to stay unbeaten since December, and most significantly, right at the top of the Championship table. With seven games to go, they were still seven points ahead of their title rivals Burnley.

'Keep going!' their captain, Wes Morgan, cried out in the dressing room. 'We're nearly there now!'

Sadly, Jamie had to miss the next home match against his beloved Sheffield Wednesday due to injury, but his team managed to win 2–1 without him.

'Great work, lads!' Jamie cheered passionately along with all the supporters at the King Power Stadium.

Their Premier League dream was getting closer and closer. In fact, they could seal their promotion the very next day, with six games to spare, if QPR and Derby both failed to win. So, with the excitement building, Jamie and some of the other Leicester players went over to watch the game together at their teammate Andy King's house.

'Yes!' they all cheered when Bournemouth took the lead against QPR just before half-time.

'No!' they groaned when QPR equalised just after the break.

'Yes!' they cheered when Bournemouth went 2–1 up.

And 'YES!' they screamed when they saw that Middlesbrough were also winning against Derby.

Leicester were now just twenty minutes away from a return to the Premier League! After an anxious wait, at last both final whistles blew, and Jamie and his teammates could get their promotion party started.

'We are going up! Say, we are going up!'

Yes, Leicester were finally back in England's top division, after ten years away. It was a massive achievement for everyone involved, but especially Jamie. Following a difficult first season, he had bounced back brilliantly, with sixteen goals and ten assists. And now his remarkable rise was set to continue. Less than three years earlier he had been a non-league footballer, and now he was about to play in the Premier League!

Jamie's injury ruled him out for the rest of the season, but he didn't really mind about that. His work was already done, and he trusted his teammates to carry on winning and secure the league title.

Campeones, Campeones, Olé! Olé! Olé!

Leicester were presented with the Championship trophy on the final day of the season at a packed King Power Stadium. Two by two, the players walked out onto the pitch as the fans clapped and cheered. The last few star performers, however, got to walk out on their own:

'Next up, he's having a party, it's… JAMIE VARDY!'

The crowd roared louder than ever as he made his way out onto the grass, wearing the full Leicester kit.

Then, with a winner's medal around his neck and an arm around Kevin's shoulder, Jamie stood and waited for Wes to lift the trophy.

3, 2, 1... Hurrrraaaaaaaaaaaaaaayyyyy!!!!!!!!

CHAPTER 16

THE GREAT ESCAPE

Jamie knew that it would be difficult to score goals in the Premier League, playing against world-class defenders every week. But after rising to every challenge so far in his remarkable career, he saw no reason why he couldn't do it again in the 2014–15 season.

'I'd back myself against anyone!' he declared confidently.

But first, Jamie had to get himself back to full fitness after his injury. He missed Leicester's first two matches against Everton and Chelsea, and then came on as a late sub against Arsenal and Stoke City. Right, now he was ready to play the full ninety minutes. It was a tough start to the season for his team, and the games weren't getting any easier. Jamie would be making his full Premier League debut at home against... Manchester United. Their team was full of famous superstars: Wayne Rooney, Robin van Persie, Falcao, Ángel Di María, David de Gea...

'Bring it on!' he told Nuge, showing no sign of fear.

Leicester manager Pearson was equally confident. He decided to go with an attacking front three: new striker, Leonardo Ulloa, in the middle, with Jamie on one side and Nuge on the other. It was a brave move, and after the first fifteen minutes, it looked like a big mistake because United were already 2–0 up and on their way to victory.

Or so they thought, until Jamie, out of nowhere, put Leicester back in the game. Getting the ball on the right, he battled his way down the wing, past the left-back Marcos Rojo, and delivered a brilliant cross into the box, just before the ball went out of play. Leonardo hardly had to move to get his head on it. *THUMP! 2–1!*

'Come on!' Jamie roared at the crowd.

In the second half, United scored a third goal, but again Leicester showed their fighting spirit. This time, Jamie popped up on the left wing to outmuscle Rafael and win the ball. Then, as he dribbled it into the box, the United right-back barged him over. *Penalty!* Up stepped Nuge to send De Gea the wrong way. *3–2!*

'Hey, we're still in this!' Jamie shouted as he high-fived his strike partner.

He was right. Two minutes later, Jamie set up Esteban Cambiasso to make it 3–3. What a comeback! The Leicester players punched the air with glee as they raced over to the corner flag to celebrate.

But Jamie wasn't done yet. After helping to create his team's first three goals, he wanted one of his own. As soon as Ritchie De Laet stole the ball off Juan Mata, Jamie was off, sprinting away from the United centre-backs and into space.

'Yes!' he called out, and Ritchie's pass was perfect. This was it; he wouldn't get a better chance to score his first Premier League goal. Jamie could sense Chris Smalling and Rooney chasing back, but they had no chance of catching him. All he had to do was hold his nerve and slide the ball past De Gea...

Goooooooooooooooooooooaaaaaaaaaaaaaaaallllllllllllllll llllllllllllll!!!!!!!!!!!!!!!!!!!!!

After his calm finish, Jamie went absolutely wild, just like all the 30,000 Leicester supporters in the stadium. He sprinted over to them and then slid across the grass on his knees. What a moment! He had come a very long way, from non-league football to scoring against one of the biggest clubs in the world.

And still Jamie wasn't finished. Tyler Blackett was the next United defender to fall victim to his speed and determination. He lunged in and fouled Jamie, just as he was about to shoot. *Penalty and a red card!* Nuge had already been subbed off, so Leonardo stepped up to take it instead. *5–3!*

Leicester were heading to a legendary win, thanks to Jamie, the star of the show. He had played his part in all five goals, scoring one and setting up four. As he left the field in the eighty-fifth minute, the crowd gave their hero a standing ovation. What a performance on his full Premier League debut!

But unfortunately, after that marvellous display

against Manchester United, things quickly went downhill for Leicester City. The Foxes failed to win a single one of their next thirteen matches, and they dropped to the bottom of the table. By Christmas, their chances of staying in the Premier League didn't look good at all.

'Going down, down, down!' the opposition supporters were singing already.

Jamie, however, wasn't going to give up yet. 'Hey, come on, we can still do this!' he urged his struggling teammates.

Jamie hadn't scored a single goal during Leicester's bad run of results, but as he had discovered during his first year in the Championship, it sometimes took time to adapt to a new level of football. He still had a lot to learn about playing against top defenders, but he was determined to prove himself in the Premier League, and prove his doubters wrong.

'Vardy's good, but he's not good enough for this division!' some people argued.

'Well, we'll see about that,' Jamie muttered under his breath as he took to the field against Tottenham.

Although Leicester had only lost one of their last three matches, they were still three points behind QPR and still in nineteenth place. With only nine games to go, the Foxes desperately needed to start winning. It wasn't going to be easy, though, and Jamie watched in horror as Tottenham took an early 2–0 lead, thanks to his old Leicester teammate, Harry Kane.

'Here we go again!' some players might have grumbled, but not Jamie. His mind was focused on finally scoring again.

As soon as he saw Nuge dribbling down the right, Jamie sprinted between Kyle Walker and Eric Dier and into the Tottenham box. He knew that his strike partner would be looking for him. When the cross came in, Jamie stretched out his left leg and guided the ball into the net. *2–1!*

Goooooooooooooooooooooaaaaaaaaaaaaaaaaalllllllllllllll llllllllllllll!!!!!!!!!!!!!!!!!!!

'Game on!' he shouted as he ran over to thank Nuge for the assist.

When Wes scored a header to make it 2–2,

the Leicester fans started dreaming about another incredible comeback. Tottenham, however, had their sights set on a Top Six finish and they fought back in style – 3–2, then 4–2. In the last minute, Jamie flicked the ball on for Nuge to make it 4–3, but it was too little too late.

'Unlucky, lads,' Pearson told his disappointed players at the final whistle. 'You showed real team spirit today. We can take a lot of positives from that game.'

Their manager was right. No, Leicester hadn't got the result they wanted against Tottenham, but it did feel like a turning point:

Leicester 2 West Ham 1,

West Brom 2 Leicester 3...

The great escape was on, and who had scored their injury-time winner? Jamie, of course! When Esteban cleared the ball towards the halfway line, he stole in front of Gareth McAuley and then set off towards the West Brom goal. As Jamie approached the penalty area, Joleon Lescott pushed him onto his left foot, but that was no problem. BANG! He blasted a beautiful shot right into the bottom corner.

Goooooooooooooooooooaaaaaaaaaaaaaaaaallllllllllllllll llllllllllllll!!!!!!!!!!!!!!!!!!!!!

Jamie had done it; he was the matchwinner, the Leicester hero. With his arms out wide, he raced over to celebrate with the supporters. 'Come onnnnnn!' he roared with passion as Nuge lifted him into the air.

Leicester were bouncing back and playing with confidence again. With a third win in a row against Swansea City, they moved off the bottom of the table, but they were still in the relegation zone. There were six games left; they just had to pick up as many points as possible...

Burnley 0 Leicester 1,

Jamie was in the right place at the right time to scramble the ball in on the goal-line.

Leicester 3 Newcastle 0,

Leicester 2 Southampton 0,

Jamie set up the second with a clever cross to Riyad Mahrez, and The Foxes moved up to sixteenth!

Sunderland 0 Leicester 0...

Their great escape was complete! At the final whistle, Jamie and his teammates huddled together on the halfway line to mark their amazing achievement. All their hard work had paid off – against the odds, Leicester would be playing in the Premier League again next year.

We are staying up! Say, we are staying up!

A week later, Leicester celebrated their safety in style by thrashing QPR 5–1. It was Jamie who grabbed the first goal, only his fifth in thirty-four games. But in the last eight matches of the season, his record stood at three goals and four assists. Just when his team needed him most, Jamie had found his top form at the top level, with the whole country watching.

CHAPTER 17

ENGLAND EXCITEMENT

Just as Jamie was thinking ahead to his well-deserved summer holiday of 2015, he received a life-changing text message, which started with the following sentence:

'You have been selected in the England senior squad for the games versus Republic of Ireland on Sunday 7 June and Slovenia on Sunday 14 June.'

Jamie's first thought was: 'Ha ha very funny, which one of my mates is joking around?' But as he read on, he began to wonder if the message might be real. There was so much detail in the text and according to the newspapers, England manager, Roy Hodgson, had been there at the Southampton match to watch him play… Jamie decided to give the Leicester physio a call, just to make sure.

'Yes, it's true, you're in – congratulations!'

Wow, so it wasn't a prank, after all – Jamie really had just been called up to play for his country. What a story, and what a proud moment for him and his family! He couldn't believe it; the news was too much to take in at first. For years, he had been an England fan, cheering them on through all the highs and lows at World Cups and Euros. But he had never dreamt that he might one day play international football himself; not since he had left Sheffield Wednesday at the age of sixteen. When he started again at Stocksbridge Park Steels, that idea had seemed impossible.

But not anymore! Once he had calmed himself down, Jamie thought back to what his agent, John Morris, had said at their very first meeting, when he was still a non-league footballer for Halifax:

'You can do whatever you want in this game. You can go on and play for England.'

Jamie had laughed at the time, but now that crazy

prediction was about to come true! Even if he did end up becoming a one-cap wonder like Nuge, he was determined to enjoy his England experience. He had definitely earned it.

Daniel Sturridge and Danny Welbeck were both out injured, while Harry Kane was still with the Under-21s, so Jamie wasn't the only new striker in Hodgson's squad. He was joined by QPR's Charlie Austin, who had also climbed the ladder from non-league football. It was nice to be able to go through the nerve-wracking training camp together. But in fact, the England team turned out to be a much friendlier environment than they had expected. Even the senior players like Rooney, Joe Hart and James Milner welcomed Jamie and Charlie into the squad and made them feel like they belonged there.

When the first matchday arrived, they sat on the subs bench together, both hoping for some game-time. With thirty minutes to go, the score was still Ireland 0 England 0, so Hodgson started to make some changes in attack. It was a friendly, so the manager could make as many substitutions as he liked. First, off came

Raheem Sterling and on came Andros Townsend, then ten minutes later, off came Wayne and on came... Jamie!

'Just do what you've been doing at Leicester,' Hodgson told him as he stood there waiting to go on.

Sure thing! Wearing the Number 21 shirt, Jamie ran and ran and ran, closing down defenders and racing into the box. Unfortunately, he didn't get any good goalscoring opportunities, but he still loved every minute of his England debut.

When would he get the chance to play for his country again? Jamie was hungry for more. Although he didn't get any more game-time in the Euro 2016 qualifier against Slovenia, he returned to Leicester feeling more motivated than ever. He was officially an international footballer now, and if he kept working hard and scoring goals for his club, hopefully he would get another England call-up soon.

When Hodgson announced his next squad in September, Jamie's name was there again. Hurray! That's because he had started the new Premier League season like he'd finished the last one, with more goals and assists. Now, it was time to switch his focus to scoring for his country.

Hodgson gave Jamie a starting spot for the first game, alongside Wayne in attack. What an opportunity! They were playing against San Marino, who had never won a competitive international match. But even though England thrashed them 6–0, Jamie found it hard to get involved in the game, and most importantly, he failed to grab his first international goal.

It was Wayne who opened the scoring from the penalty spot, equalling the England record. Jamie could have set his strike partner up for his record-breaking goal, but he lost his composure at the crucial moment.

'Arghhh!' he screamed up at the sky.

It just wasn't Jamie's day. He chased after a throughball, but the keeper came out and beat him to the ball. He tried to pick out Alex Oxlade-Chamberlain in the box, but his cross was too high. As the game went on, Jamie grew more and more frustrated with himself. He even started a silly argument with one of the San Marino defenders. Then, to make matters worse, Theo Walcott and Harry Kane both came on as second-half subs and scored.

Each time, Jamie jogged over to congratulate his teammates, but in his head, he couldn't help thinking, 'That should have been me!'

The BBC website gave him a rating of 6 out of 10: 'Worked his socks off and was aggressive, but not everything worked.'

Oh dear, had Jamie blown his big chance with England? For their second match against Switzerland, he found himself back on the bench. And when the team needed a winning goal, Hodgson turned to Harry instead, who scored almost immediately.

Oh well – Jamie would just have to keep playing well for Leicester and hope for more opportunities to prove himself at international level.

CHAPTER 18

A RECORD-BREAKING RUN

As he entered the Stoke City box, Jamie took a second to steady himself, before firing a shot just over the diving keeper.

Goooooooooooooooooooooaaaaaaaaaaaaaaaaalllllllllllllll llllllllllll!!!!!!!!!!!!!!!!!!!!

The Leicester fans rose to their feet, ready to serenade their star striker with a brand-new song:

Jamie Vardy, he scores when he wants!

It was true; he had now found the net in three games in a row, leading his team up to third in the Premier League table, behind only the two Manchester clubs. Not bad for 'one of the worst teams in the league'.

At the start of the 2015–16 season, most people had made Leicester favourites for relegation, but that only made the players more determined to prove everyone wrong. The rest of the league was in for a surprise when they faced Leicester City, that was for sure. Although Pearson had been replaced by new Italian manager, Claudio Ranieri, the team spirit was stronger than ever, and so was the squad. The Foxes now had Robert Huth and Christian Fuchs alongside Wes in defence, N'Golo Kanté alongside Danny Drinkwater in midfield, Shinji Okazaki alongside Jamie, and Leonardo and Riyad in an attack that combined speed and skill.

'Don't worry, I'm not here to change the style of play,' Ranieri reassured the players as soon as he arrived. 'I just want you to keep playing the same way you did at the end of last season.'

And so far, the plan was working perfectly. Well, almost perfectly. In their next game, Leicester lost 5–2 against Arsenal, but even in defeat, the team showed real fighting spirit. Especially Jamie, whose confidence was sky-high. Racing onto Danny's ball over the top, he dribbled into the box and calmly curled a shot into the far corner before an Arsenal defender could close him down.

Goooooooooooooooooooaaaaaaaaaaaaaaaalllllllllllllll llllllllllllll!!!!!!!!!!!!!!!!!!!!

Jamie threw his arms out wide and listened to the home fans chanting his name. It was a feeling that never got old, no matter how many times it happened. And it was happening a lot these days! In his second season in the Premier League, Leicester's Number 9 was scoring goal after goal, game after game:

A penalty against Norwich,

Then two more against Southampton!

Jamie's first goal was a glancing header and the second was a powerful right-foot finish from Riyad's throughball.

'Mate, you're unstoppable at the moment!' Danny cheered as they celebrated another fantastic Leicester fightback.

Jamie had now scored in six games in a row, and he kept his remarkable run going by scoring the winner against Crystal Palace a week later. It was his tenth goal of the season already, and he raised both hands to show the crowd. What a season he was having! Now, Jamie stepped out onto the football pitch, expecting to score every time. And he did, against:

West Brom,

Watford,

And Newcastle.

From wide on the left wing, Jamie passed infield to Leonardo and then raced forward for the one-two. But when the return pass arrived, he found his path blocked by Moussa Sissoko. No problem; not when he was in such fine form! In a flash, Jamie cut inside past Sissoko and squeezed a shot in at the keeper's near post. *1–0!*

Gooooooooooooooooooooaaaaaaaaaaaaaaaallllllllllllll lllllllllllll!!!!!!!!!!!!!!!!!!!

As the ball hit the back of the net, Jamie just kept running, all the way to the corner flag, blowing kisses to the crowd. Ten games in a row! He had just equalled Ruud van Nistelrooy's Premier League record.

'Well done, Vards!' Wes shouted, lifting his

teammate high into the air.

So, could Jamie go on and break the record, by scoring in an eleventh consecutive game? 'Of course I can!' he declared confidently, but he knew it wouldn't be that easy. Because Leicester's next game was against… Manchester United.

'Oh well, I scored against De Gea last season, so I can do it again today,' Jamie told his teammates.

Still, the pressure was really on him this time. Nike had sent Jamie a special pair of gold boots to wear in the match, and van Nistelrooy had even sent him a 'Good Luck!' message on social media. As kick-off approached, it was all anyone was talking about.

Will Vardy do it? Can he make it eleven games in a row?

Jamie tried his best to treat it just like any other match, like any of his ten previous games for Leicester. But the excitement was hard to ignore. One more goal – that was all he needed to go down in Premier League history.

'Come on, you can do it, Vards!' Wes told him as the Leicester team walked out in front of a sell-out crowd at the King Power Stadium. 'We're behind you all the way!'

In the third minute, Shinji tried to cross the ball to Jamie in the middle, but Chris Smalling made the interception.

'Oooooooooohhhh,' the home fans groaned. Nearly!

Ten minutes later, Jamie got the ball just inside the United box.

'Shoot! Shoot!' the supporters urged, but in the end he passed to N'Golo instead.

Jamie had to be patient and wait for the perfect opportunity to arrive. It came in the twenty-fourth minute, as Kasper caught the ball straight from a corner-kick and launched another one of their classic counter-attacks. He rolled the ball quickly out to Christian, who did what the Leicester defenders usually did – look up and look for Jamie on the run. There he was, racing from one side of the pitch to the other and pointing to the space behind the United left-back…

'Yes, now!'

Christian's pass was perfect, allowing Jamie to skip past Matteo Darmian with ease. He was one on one with De Gea now, who rushed out towards him, making his body as big as possible. Every Leicester fan at home and in the stadium held their breath as Jamie took the shot. Was this it, the moment they had all been waiting for? His powerful strike flew past De Gea's outstretched leg and into the bottom corner.

Gooooooooooooooooooooaaaaaaaaaaaaaaaaallllllllllllll llllllllllll!!!!!!!!!!!!!!!!!!!

Jamie reacted with pure delight and raw emotion. 'Me! Me! Me!' he roared, pointing at his chest again and again as he sprinted past the supporters and into Christian's arms. Yes, he had done it; he had scored in eleven games in a row. Only four years ago Jamie had been playing non-league football and now he was a new Premier League record holder. What an astonishing achievement! As he ran back for the restart, he heard a familiar song ring out around the King Power Stadium:

Jamie Vardy, he scores when he wants!

Could life get any better than this?

CHAPTER 19

THE
UNBELIEVABLES

Yes, it turned out life could get even better for Jamie,
and for his Leicester teammates too. Their match
against Manchester United finished in a 1–1 draw,
putting The Foxes joint top of the table. And after two
more wonderful wins against Chelsea and Everton,
Leicester moved two points clear as the new Premier
League leaders!

Of their first seventeen games in that 2015–16
season, they had only lost one, so instead of fighting
relegation, they were now fighting for the title. It was
an unbelievable turnaround. At the start of the season,
the odds on Leicester winning the league had been
5000–1! But suddenly, that didn't sound like such a

silly bet, after all…

'No, there's no way they can keep this up,' argued many of the journalists and the football pundits on TV. 'They'll start slipping up after Christmas.'

But no, after going three games without a victory, Leicester bounced back stronger than ever. Jamie was still scoring regularly but winning was now even more of a team effort. At the back, Kasper, Wes and Robert were keeping clean sheet after clean sheet, and in attack, they were sharing the goals around. Robert headed home the winner at Tottenham, Shinji scored against Aston Villa, and Danny and Leonardo found the net against Stoke.

'Come on, we can do this!' Leicester's band of brothers in blue cried out together.

They were three points clear at the top, but still people didn't really believe in them. 'First, let's see how they do in their next two games,' the pundits said.

Liverpool at home, then Manchester City away – it really was make or break for Leicester's Premier League title challenge, but the players were ready and raring to go. They weren't scared of anyone, and they were taking things one game at a time.

First, Liverpool...

With sixty minutes gone, the game was still goalless. They were struggling to create clear chances and the crowd was starting to grow restless.

Leicester, Leicester, LEICESTER!

What they needed was a moment of pure magic...

As Riyad got the ball deep in his own half, he only had one thought on his mind – find Jamie for the quick counter-attack. So he sent a long, looping pass over the Liverpool defence for his teammate to chase.

Jamie reached the ball first, of course, but he didn't have much time. He could see Dejan Lovren racing over to stop him and Mamadou Sakho too. Plus, Simon Mignolet was moving back towards his goal line, so it was now or never...

As the ball bounced up off the grass, Jamie watched it carefully and then hit it first time on the half-volley. Why not, with the sensational season he was having? *BANG!*

What a strike! Jamie stood and watched from the

edge of the area as the ball flew over Mignolet's up-stretched arms and into the back of the net. *1–0!*

Goooooooooooooooooooaaaaaaaaaaaaaaaallllllllllllll llllllllllll!!!!!!!!!!!!!!!!!!!!

'Get in!' Jamie roared, buzzing with excitement as he ran over to the home fans by the corner flag. It was one of his best strikes ever and what a time to score it!

And ten minutes later, he added a second goal to secure another wonderful Leicester win. Shinji slipped just as he was about to shoot, but as the ball rolled across the six-yard box, Jamie pounced like a proper Premier League striker. *2–0!*

'Well done, great team effort today,' Ranieri congratulated each and every one of his players after the final whistle. 'Now, onto the next match!'

…then, Manchester City…

Winning away at the Etihad was supposed to be their toughest test yet, but in the end, Leicester made it look easy. Robert opened the scoring in only the third minute, and he grabbed another goal early in the second half to make it 3–0.

'Huthy, you hero!' Jamie yelled as he chased after

the centre-back.

Leicester just would not be beaten. This was *their* season, no doubt about it.

'Premier League Champions, here we come!' the players cheered together at the final whistle. Their team spirit was so strong that no-one could stop them.

Or could they? With ten games to go, Tottenham were closing in; they were now only three points behind them. The Leicester players had to hold their nerve, staying solid at the back and lethal on the counter-attack:

Watford 0 Leicester 1,

Leicester 1 Newcastle 0...

'Vardy wins the header at the back post and there's Okazaki with the acrobatic overhead kick – GOAL!'

...Crystal Palace 0 Leicester 1...

'Vardy teases the defender, going one way then the other, and then crosses it to Mahrez – GOAL!'

...Leicester 1 Southampton 0,

Sunderland 0 Leicester 2...

'A long ball forward from Drinkwater, and he's released Vardy, who makes no mistake – GOAL!'

Jamie was up to twenty-one goals for the season and The Foxes were now seven points clear at the top of the table! They were really close now. The players had shown so much passion and desire all season, and they just had to keep going and finish what they had started. One last push and that title would be theirs.

In their next game against West Ham, Leicester got off to the perfect start with a classic team counter-attack. Kasper rolled the ball out to Riyad, who passed to N'Golo, who dribbled forward and then slipped it through to Jamie.

The Leicester fans rose to their feet in anticipation. They knew exactly what to expect when their star striker got the ball in the box. Right foot or left foot – it didn't matter because Jamie was deadly with both, and from any angle. It was always the same story:

BANG!... Goooooooooooooooaaaaaaaaaaaaaaaalllll llllllllllllllllllllllll!!!!!!!!!!!!!!!!!!!!

'Yesssssssss!' Jamie roared at the crowd, raising his arms up like a champion already.

After that major high, however, he came crashing back down to earth. He had already received a yellow card in the first half, when he fell over in the box and appealed, 'Penalty!'

But to Jamie's surprise, the referee awarded a free kick to West Ham and showed him a second yellow card for diving, followed by a red.

'What, you can't be serious?' Jamie asked innocently, but his shock soon turned to fury. 'Ref, you're sending me off? What a ridiculous decision!' he snarled before storming off the pitch.

Down to ten men for the last thirty minutes, Leicester managed to hold on for a 2–2 draw. The good news was that result took them one point closer to the title. But the bad news was that Jamie would have to miss their next two important matches because of his angry reaction to the red card.

'Sorry, lads,' he apologised to his teammates for letting them down.

'Don't worry,' Wes reassured him. 'We'll get the job done without you, just you watch!'

And they did:

Leicester 4 Swansea 0,
Manchester United 1 Leicester 1...

'Well done, lads!' Jamie cheered as he walked around the dressing room at Old Trafford, congratulating everyone. 'What a team performance!'

That one point meant that if Tottenham didn't beat Chelsea the following day, Leicester would be crowned the new Premier League Champions.

'Hey, any of you lot want to watch the game at my house tomorrow?' Jamie asked, thinking back to two years earlier, when they had celebrated promotion from the Championship together at Andy's.

In the end, most of the Leicester squad squeezed into Jamie's living room to share a moment they would never forget. From 2–0 up at half-time, Tottenham collapsed to a 2–2 draw.

'Leicester City,' the commentator on TV confirmed, 'are Champions of the Premier League.'

They had done it; the favourites for relegation had gone all the way and won the title. Unbelievable! Thanks to their amazing mix of teamwork, talent and belief, the Leicester players had made a football fairytale come true.

Campeones, Campeones, Olé! Olé! Olé!

Their party went on all night and it continued at the King Power Stadium a few days later, along with 30,000 screaming fans. After a 3–1 win over Everton, featuring another two goals from Jamie, it was time for the Premier League trophy presentation. One by one, Leicester's heroes walked out onto the pitch, high-fiving everyone they passed:

Kasper,

Then Danny,

Then Robert,

Then Jamie...

'Hi!' he waved proudly up at his friends and family in the crowd. 'We did it!'

Once they'd collected their winner's medals, the players all gathered on the stage, waiting for Wes and Ranieri to raise the trophy together.

3, 2, 1... Hurrrraaaaaaaaaaaaaayyyyy!!!!!!!

As fireworks and blue confetti filled the sky above the stadium, Wes passed the trophy along the line of teammates. When it finally came to Jamie, he gave it a quick kiss and then lifted it high above his head. 'Come onnnnnnn!'

It was only then that the significance of what he'd achieved really began to sink in. Just four years after leaving non-league football to turn professional, Jamie was now a Premier League champion!

CHAPTER 20

A MIXED EXPERIENCE AT EURO 2016

For Jamie, the next few weeks were a happy blur of parties, photos, and open-top bus parades. His club, Leicester City, were the Premier League Champions, and he was enjoying every moment of it. Although he lost out to Harry Kane in the race to win the Golden Boot, Jamie didn't feel too disappointed because he was named Premier League Player of the Season instead!

And the biggest year of his life wasn't over yet. When Hodgson named his England squad of twenty-three for Euro 2016, he selected six forwards on the list:

Wayne Rooney, Raheem Sterling, Harry Kane,

Daniel Sturridge, Marcus Rashford and… JAMIE VARDY.

Incredible – it was another crazy dream come true; at the age of twenty-nine, Jamie was off to play for his country in his first international tournament! He knew that he probably wouldn't be England's starting striker – that would be Wayne or Harry – but he had already shown his manager that he could make a big impact off the bench.

Earlier that year, Jamie had been England's super sub in an amazing away win in Germany. When he came on to replace Danny Welbeck, his team had been losing 2–1, but just three minutes later, they were level. As Nathaniel Clyne dribbled up the right wing, Jamie ran through the middle, waiting for the perfect moment to… *ZOOM!* When the cross came in, he sprinted towards the front post, flicking the ball past the keeper with a brilliant back-heel.

Goooooooooooooooooooaaaaaaaaaaaaaaaaallllllllllllll llllllllllll!!!!!!!!!!!!!!!!!!!

Jamie breathed a sigh of relief as he raced over to Nathaniel with his arms out wide. At last, he had his first England goal and what a way to score it! It was a moment of magic that proved all his doubters wrong; of course, he was good enough to play for his country.

'That was pure class!' Jordan Henderson cheered as they celebrated together.

And three days later, Jamie showed his quality again by scoring another against the Netherlands. Two in two! So, could he now go on and become England's super sub at Euro 2016? That was the aim as the squad set off for France.

Jamie didn't get to play in their first group game against Russia, but he came on at half-time in their second against Wales. England were losing 1–0 and they needed to win, so Hodgson put another lethal striker on the pitch...

Jamie's job was to cause as many problems as possible for the Welsh defence, and he did it brilliantly. From the moment the second half started, he was constantly on the move. When Wayne's cross looped up into the air, Jamie was there in the penalty area, battling bravely for the flick-on. Eventually, Wales managed to scramble it away, but only as far as

Daniel, England's other substitute. His cross caused chaos in the six-yard box, and as the ball bounced, Jamie pounced. *BANG!*

Gooooooooooooooooooooaaaaaaaaaaaaaaaaalllllllllllllll llllllllllll!!!!!!!!!!!!!!!!!!!!!

England had equalised, and it was all thanks to their super subs. 'Come onnnnnnn!' Jamie roared with passion and pride as he raced over to celebrate by the bench. A crucial goal for England at the Euros – it was easily one of the greatest moments of his amazing football adventure. It didn't matter whether he was playing for club or country; Jamie just couldn't stop scoring!

'Nice one, Vards!' Wayne cried out. 'Now, let's get another!'

Although it wasn't Jamie who scored the winner, he played a key part yet again. Deep in injury time, Daniel launched one last attack; it was now or never for England. As the pass arrived, Jamie had his back to goal in the Wales box, so he played a quick, clever ball across to Dele Alli. Dele went down, calling for a penalty, but it didn't matter because Daniel had

continued his run into exactly the right area to poke a
shot past the keeper. *2–1!*

'Yessssssssss!' Wayne screamed into the camera as
the whole team celebrated together. It was England's
super subs to the rescue!

As a reward for their efforts, Jamie and Daniel both
got to start in the final group game against Slovakia.
However, as hard as they tried, they couldn't become
England heroes again, and the match ended in a
disappointing 0–0 draw. Walking off the pitch, Jamie
couldn't help thinking about his wasted opportunities,
especially a one-on-one in the first half, which the
keeper had saved. 'How did I miss that?' he groaned
in disbelief. 'I score those every time for Leicester!'

For England's Round of 16 match against Iceland,
Harry was back in attack and Jamie was back on the
bench. However, in the sixtieth minute, Hodgson
had to call upon his super sub again. England were
2–1 down and heading out of the tournament, unless
someone could save them…

'I can do this!' Jamie told himself as he raced on
to replace Raheem. But despite his confidence and

tireless running, it turned out to be a very frustrating night for everyone in an England shirt. Nothing went right, and everything went wrong.

When Harry played a dangerous through ball for him to chase, Jamie's first touch was too heavy, allowing the defender to make the tackle.

'Sorry – great pass, H!'

When Daniel curled a lovely cross into the box, Jamie looked like he was going to win the header, but at the last moment, his marker outjumped him.

'Arghhh!'

Jamie won his next header, but his flick-on flew past Harry and into the Iceland keeper's arms.

'Noooo!'

In the ninetieth minute, Jamie made one last run to reach Marcus's corner-kick, but his shot was blocked.

'NOOOOO!'

Moments later, it was all over – England 1 Iceland 2. They were heading home, even before the quarter-finals. They had been knocked out of Euro 2016 by a national team ranked thirty-fourth in the world. How embarrassing, and what a disaster!

'That's the worst performance I've ever seen from an England team,' Alan Shearer declared on TV.

After the final whistle, Jamie walked around the pitch in a state of shock. From the ecstatic high of scoring against Wales, his Euro 2016 experience had ended on the lowest of lows. With the whole country counting on them, England's players had failed. That was a horrible feeling, the worst of his football career. Jamie just hoped that he would get another chance to make his country proud at World Cup 2018.

CHAPTER 21

NO ONE-SEASON WONDER!

By the time Jamie returned to England, the transfer rumours were flying. Suddenly, all the top teams wanted to sign Leicester's title-winning stars. Chelsea were chasing N'Golo, Danny was possibly moving back to Manchester United, while Jamie and Riyad were both attracting interest from Arsenal.

Arsenal! Wow, it was nice to know that such a big club wanted to sign him. They were even willing to pay £20 million. Mesut Özil, Alexis Sánchez, Theo Walcott – the Gunners had lots of skill and speed in attack, but they didn't have a natural goalscorer, a star striker like Jamie.

'If I was Vardy, I'd say yes to Arsenal straight away,'

a lot of people argued. 'This is his big opportunity, and he's not getting any younger.'

'Yeah, and he's probably a one-season wonder anyway, just like Leicester.'

But no, Jamie wasn't going to turn his back on the club that had always believed in him, even during his difficult early days in the Championship. So instead of joining Arsenal, Jamie stayed loyal and signed a new four-year contract at Leicester.

'What we achieved last season was beyond what anyone could have imagined,' he told the media, 'but we've got to go again. We're defending the title and we've got the Champions League to look forward to.'

Jamie couldn't wait to take on his latest challenge – European football. He had grown up watching the big games on TV, but now as a Premier League champion, he would be playing in them! In the group stage, Leicester faced Club Brugge, FC Copenhagen and Porto.

'Bring it on, we can beat all of those teams!' Jamie declared confidently.

And they did – Leicester won all three home games

as they finished top of Group G. That was terrific
news for the team, but Jamie still hadn't scored a
single Champions League goal, and he was struggling
in the Premier League too. Aside from a stunning hat-
trick against Manchester City, Jamie had only scored
twice in twenty-one matches. Oh dear, was he going
to be a one-season wonder after all?

It looked that way for the Leicester team too.
Following a run of five defeats in a row, The Foxes
dropped down to seventeenth place, just one point
above the relegation zone. So, with a heavy heart, the
club sacked their manager, Ranieri, and replaced him
with his assistant, Craig Shakespeare. The plan was
for the team to return to their old, counter-attacking
ways, and it worked immediately, for Jamie in
particular.

Liverpool were in for a surprise when they arrived
at the King Power Stadium because the old Leicester
were back! As soon as Marc Albrighton got the ball
in midfield, he looked up and slid it through to his
striker. His pass was perfect and so was Jamie's run,
in between the centre-backs, who had no chance of

catching him. He was one-on-one with the keeper now – could he keep his cool and score? Of course he could! Jamie steadied himself and then placed his shot right in the bottom corner.

Goooooooooooooooooooooaaaaaaaaaaaaaaaalllllllllllllll llllllllllll!!!!!!!!!!!!!!!!!!!!

'Yesssssss!' he roared as he slid on his knees towards the corner flag. After a very frustrating first half of the season, Jamie finally felt back to his best. And to prove it, he scored again in the second half, heading home from Christian's excellent cross. 3–0!

No way was Jamie just a one-season wonder! At last, he was scoring lots of goals again:

With his left foot against West Ham, Sunderland, and Crystal Palace,

And with his right foot against Stoke City, West Brom, and Bournemouth.

'Yes, Vards – you're back!' Danny yelled as Leicester climbed up to mid-table.

And Jamie wasn't just performing well in the Premier League; he was also now starring in the Champions League too. Racing onto Danny's cross, he smashed a shot past the Sevilla keeper to score for the first time in Europe and give Leicester an all-important away goal.

'Come on, we can win this!'

Then in the second leg of Leicester's quarter-final against Atlético Madrid, Jamie reacted first to the loose ball. The six-yard box was crowded with the keeper and five defenders, but none of them could block Jamie's calm, clever finish into the top corner.

Goooooooooooooooooooooaaaaaaaaaaaaaaaaaalllllllllllllll llllllllllll!!!!!!!!!!!!!!!!!!!!

Leicester 1 Atlético 2 – the comeback was on!

'Let's go!' Jamie yelled, grabbing the ball, and urging the home fans to make more noise.

Sadly, as hard as they tried, The Foxes couldn't find an equaliser, and so their extraordinary Champions League adventure ended at the quarter-final stage. Long after the final whistle had blown, Jamie lay sprawled out flat on the grass, exhausted and absolutely gutted. It was a horrible feeling to know that the team had given everything and come so close, but eventually, Jamie picked himself up and left the pitch. He was one of Leicester's senior players now, and the youngsters looked up to him. It was time to lead by example.

'Hey, we should be proud of what we've achieved this year.' Jamie tried his best to lift the spirits in the disappointed dressing room. 'Now, we just have to work hard and make sure there's a next time.'

Jamie started the 2017–18 season like a man on a serious mission: to fire Leicester back into the Premier League Top Four and then back into the Champions League. He scored two against Arsenal, then one against Chelsea and Liverpool. It was yet more proof that he was a big game player; no-one could call Jamie a 'one-season wonder' anymore! Unfortunately, however, Leicester only won one of their first eight matches and by the end of October, they were at risk of being relegated again. So, the club decided it was time for another new manager.

At first, Leicester looked better with Claude Puel in charge, but before long, it was back to the same old story. Their star striker kept scoring, but the team weren't winning enough matches. By the end of the season, Jamie had again reached twenty Premier League goals, while helping Leicester to finish in a respectable ninth place.

There was no time to sit back and enjoy a well-deserved rest, however. Instead, Jamie had to quickly switch his focus from club to country because his goals had earned him a place in the England squad for the 2018 World Cup! For Jamie, it was yet another childhood dream come true.

'What an honour!' he posted on social media. 'No words to describe the feeling right now..... Can't wait to get going! See you in Russia.'

Since their embarrassing exit at Euro 2016, England had made significant changes under new manager, Gareth Southgate. As well as a new 3–5–2 formation, there was also now a really fun, friendly atmosphere around the squad. Everyone got on really well with each other, no matter what Premier League club they played for, which led to better performances and a lot more positivity. Plus, with less pressure on them to win the World Cup this time, the players could go to Russia, do their best and enjoy themselves.

Jamie felt proud and happy to be a part of the new-look England squad, even though he was still used as a super sub. If Harry and Raheem needed help up front, he was ready and waiting to come on and make his country proud...

For England's opening group game against Tunisia, Jamie was an anxious spectator, cheering from the bench as Harry headed home a last-minute winner. Phew! Thankfully, their second match against Panama was a lot more straightforward. Midway through the second half, England were already 6–1 up, and so Southgate sent on Jamie to make his World Cup debut.

What a moment! But for all his running and battling, Jamie couldn't grab a first World Cup goal against Panama,

Or in the 1–0 loss against Belgium five days later,

Or in England's penalty shoot-out win over Colombia,

Or in the devastating 2–1 defeat to Croatia, which ended England's amazing World Cup adventure.

'Gutted,' Jamie wrote on Twitter afterwards, along

with a message to all the amazing supporters who had helped make it such a special tournament. 'Thank you to every one of you who have been there each step of the way!'

Although he hadn't been able to save England from a semi-final defeat, Jamie knew that playing for his country at the 2018 World Cup was still an experience that he would never, ever forget.

CHAPTER 22

ON FIRE FOR THE FOXES AGAIN!

Once the tournament was over, Jamie took some time off to relax and reflect on his remarkable journey so far. In the space of six incredible years, he had gone from non-league footballer to Premier League champion and World Cup star with England. So, what would happen next in his sensational story? Jamie couldn't wait to find out, and after a week of rest with his family, he was raring to go again for Leicester.

'Come on, let's show everyone we're a Top-Six team!' he urged his teammates.

Although Riyad had moved on to Manchester City, the Leicester squad looked stronger than ever. The club had signed Jonny Evans and Çağlar Söyüncü to play alongside Wes and Harry Maguire in defence, as well as a rampaging right back called Ricardo Pereira and a classy midfield playmaker called James Maddison.

So, expectations were high as the 2018–19 Premier League season started, but they didn't last long. Despite Jamie scoring yet another goal against Manchester United, Leicester lost the match 2–1, and they lost to Liverpool, Bournemouth, Everton, and Arsenal too. With ten games played, The Foxes were twelfth in the table, and they were still there seventeen games later.

'Not good enough,' Jamie muttered, shaking his head with anger and frustration after an awful 4–1 defeat to Crystal Palace.

Manager Puel had tried to switch Leicester's style of play, but it really wasn't working. Slow passing and lots of possession didn't suit Jamie's talents at all. With his speed, he wanted quick through-balls to chase on the counter-attack.

'That's how we won the league!' he grumbled.

Fortunately for Jamie and his team, things

were about to change. Three days after their poor performance against Palace, the club appointed a new manager. Brendan Rodgers had been very successful at Swansea, Liverpool and Celtic, so could he do the same at Leicester?

'Together, we'll be stronger and I'm looking forward to working with the players, staff and supporters to make the right steps forward,' their new manager told the media.

One of those steps was to develop a strong relationship with the club's star striker.

'I'm really glad you're here,' Rodgers said, shaking Jamie's hand. 'You're my kind of player – passion, energy, and a hunger to score. I'm here to help get you firing again!'

All of a sudden, Leicester were back on the counter-attack, and Jamie was back to his best. When new signing Youri Tielemans slipped a ball through for him to chase, he sprinted in between the Watford centre-backs, before lifting a shot over the keeper.

Goooooooooooooooooooooaaaaaaaaaaaaaaaaallllllllllllll lllllllllllll!!!!!!!!!!!!!!!!!!!!!

'Yes, that's more like it!' Jamie shouted as he slid towards the corner flag to celebrate.

A week later against Fulham, he set up the first goal for Youri and then raced through to score two more of his own, thanks to assists from James and Harvey Barnes. The Leicester attack was linking up wonderfully now, making Jamie more lethal than ever:

A header against Bournemouth,

A tap-in and a spot-kick against Huddersfield,

A clever poke past the keeper against West Ham...

'Yessssssss!'

After a few frustrating seasons, Jamie was really loving life at Leicester again and he couldn't stop scoring. His record under Rodgers stood at seven goals in seven games so far, and there were two more to come at the King Power Stadium against Arsenal.

Youri had given Leicester the lead in the sixtieth minute, but 1–0 was always a nerve-wracking scoreline, especially against a top team like Arsenal. Could they hold on? Jonny and Harry were defending brilliantly at the back, but a second goal would help make their job a lot easier...

When Kasper unleashed a long goal kick downfield, Jamie was as alert as ever and ready to run. *ZOOM!* It was time for another classic Leicester counter-attack. As the ball flew over his head, Jamie turned and chased after it, sprinting away from the struggling Arsenal centre-backs. It was just him and the out-rushing keeper now, so Jamie went for the lob. It looked like the ball was looping down into the top corner but instead, it crashed back off the crossbar. Luckily, however, Jamie had followed his shot in and so he was there in the six-yard box to head the rebound into the empty net. 2–0!

Gooooooooooooooooooaaaaaaaaaaaaaaaalllllllllllll llllllllllll!!!!!!!!!!!!!!!!!!

'Nice one, Vards!' Youri cheered, giving him a big hug.

Not only were they now winning 2–0, but it was also Jamie's ninety-ninth league goal for Leicester, in both the Championship and the Premier League. And he still had ten minutes left to make it one hundred...

In the last seconds, Ricardo burst into the box and cut the ball back to where he knew his striker would

be – around the penalty spot, just waiting to pounce.
BANG!... 3–0!

*Goooooooooooooooooooaaaaaaaaaaaaaaaalllllllllllll
llllllllllll!!!!!!!!!!!!!!!!!!!*

Jamie had done it – one hundred league goals
for Leicester! He ran over to Ricardo and lifted him
high into the air. 'Thanks, mate!' As Jamie knew so
well, winning was a team effort and Leicester looked
the real deal now. They had quality players in every
position, as well as a strong squad spirit again.

The Foxes finished the 2018–19 Premier League
season in ninth place, but the following year, they
would be aiming a lot higher. Yes, Leicester's target for
2020 would be the Top Four.

CHAPTER 23

GOING FOR THE GOLDEN BOOT

Jamie couldn't wait for the 2019–20 season to start, especially after seeing who Leicester's third opponents would be: Sheffield United! Oh boy, beating his beloved Wednesday's big local rivals would be the perfect way to really kick off the new campaign after two decent draws.

'Let's win this, lads!' he urged his teammates in the dressing room, more determined than ever.

Just as the first half was coming to an end, James Maddison played an excellent pass to set Jamie free. He was off, racing into the box, where he finished in style with his left foot.

Goooooooooooaaaaaaaaaaaaalllllllllllllllllllll!!!!!!!!!!!!!

Jamie couldn't resist the chance to wind up the United supporters, so he stood in front of them, cheekily cupping his ears, as if to say, 'Sorry, I can't hear you! Can you be a bit louder?'

From there, Jamie's season of scoring goals just got better and better:

Two against Bournemouth,

Two against Newcastle,

And then three against Southampton!

Wow, he was up to nine goals already, after only ten games. Could this finally be the year when Jamie won the Premier League Golden Boot? He had finished second in 2016 when it was awarded to Harry Kane, and then fourth in 2018 when it was awarded to Mo Salah, but this time, they were both trailing behind him. Still, Jamie knew that scoring wasn't everything in football.

'Winning matches,' he told his teammates, 'that's the most important thing for me.'

And Leicester were doing exactly that. With eight wins in a row between October and December, The Foxes were now second in the Premier League table.

'Champions League, here we come again!' the players celebrated together.

Jamie, meanwhile, was up to sixteen goals for the season in only sixteen games. If he got the chance to shoot, he was simply unstoppable! He had also scored in eight matches in a row, putting him just three games away from equalling the Premier League record that he had set himself back in 2015. Could he go even further this time?

Unfortunately not. Sadly, he couldn't keep his great form going, and neither could Leicester. Due to surprise defeats against Southampton and Burnley, they dropped down to third place, and Chelsea and Manchester United were catching up quickly.

'Come on, we can't let this slip!' Rodgers urged his players.

At last, after going seven games without scoring, Jamie bounced back against Aston Villa. His first goal was a penalty, and his second was a quick reaction strike into the bottom corner.

'Yesssssssss!' Jamie roared, jumping up in front of the fans to punch the air with passion. He had missed that fantastic scoring feeling.

That was Jamie's nineteenth goal of the season. And, more importantly, his ninety-ninth in the Premier League. Only twenty-eight other players had ever made it all the way to a hundred, and he was so close to joining the very exclusive club.

'Get ready for another party next week!' Jamie joked with his teammates at training, but that victory over Villa turned out to be their last match for a long time. The season had to be suspended due to COVID-19 and no-one was sure when or if they would be able to finish it.

Noooo. Would Jamie's amazing achievement have to wait until next season? Not only was he sitting on ninety-nine Premier League goals, but he was also leading the race to win the 2019–20 Golden Boot. With nineteen goals, he was two ahead of Arsenal's Pierre-Emerick Aubameyang, three ahead of Salah and Manchester City's Sergio Agüero, and four ahead of Southampton's Danny Ings.

Oh well, as much as Jamie wanted to win the award, people's health was far more important. So as the days and months passed, he waited patiently for it to be safe to play football again. He spent the time at home with his family, helping the kids with their schoolwork and growing vegetables in the garden.

At last, Jamie got the good news he was waiting for – the Premier League season would be restarting in June! But there was bad news too – supporters would not be allowed in to watch the matches, so Jamie would just have to his enjoy his special moment in an empty stadium. Well, that was if he managed to score...

Jamie couldn't grab his hundredth Premier League goal in Leicester's first match back against Watford,

Or their second against Brighton,

Or their third against Everton.

'Come on, mate,' Jamie's friends joked. 'Stop keeping us waiting and score!'

At last, in July, the party arrived in Leicester's fourth match against Crystal Palace. They were already winning 1–0 when suddenly Mamadou Sakho slipped on the left side of his own box. Harvey was onto the loose ball in a flash, and he knew who would be waiting in the middle for the cross – Jamie. With the side of his right foot, he guided the ball into the back of the net.

Goooooooooooooooooooooaaaaaaaaaaaaaaaaalllllllllllllll llllllllllllll!!!!!!!!!!!!!!!!!!!!

It was a good thing all the Premier League players had been tested for the coronavirus because Jamie couldn't help but hug Harvey and then let out a long, loud cry of joy and relief. Finally, his wait was over – he had his one hundredth Premier League goal, and he was so proud of his achievement.

'Yes, you did it, Vards!' Youri yelled as he rushed over to join in the celebrations.

With one target reached, Jamie moved onto the other: going for the Golden Boot.

He added a late second goal against Palace – twenty-one,

Then yet another against Arsenal – twenty-two,

And a tap-in against Bournemouth – twenty-three.

Would that be enough goals to get the Golden Boot? Jamie hoped so, but he still had one last game to go. It was a massive match as well, Leicester vs

Manchester United, and whoever won it would finish fourth and claim the last Champions League place.

Sadly, it wasn't to be for Leicester. Despite their hard work all season, they were defeated and slipped down to fifth place. At the final whistle, Jamie felt absolutely gutted, but at least he had some good news to ease the pain. Aubameyang and Ings had both finished on twenty-two for the season, so with twenty-three goals, the winner of the 2019–20 Premier League Golden Boot was...

'JAMIE VARDY!'

It was yet another amazing moment in his incredible football journey. When his Sheffield Wednesday dream ended at the age of sixteen, Jamie had almost given up on playing the game altogether. But instead, he had used his speed, his shooting skills, and his sheer determination to work his way up from playing non-league football while working in a factory to becoming a Leicester legend and an England international, not to mention a Premier League Champion, record-breaker and now Golden Boot winner too. It was an astonishing story, and it wasn't over yet. No – Jamie Vardy still had plenty more goals to score and targets to achieve.

JAMIE VARDY HONOURS

FC Halifax Town
🏆 Northern Premier League Premier Division:
2010–11

Fleetwood Town
🏆 Conference Premier: 2011–12

Leicester City
🏆 Championship: 2013–14
🏆 Premier League: 2015–16

Individual

🏆 Conference Premier Top Goalscorer: 2011–12

🏆 Premier League Player of the Season: 2015–16

🏆 FWA Footballer of the Year: 2015–16

🏆 PFA Premier League Team of the Year: 2015–16, 2019–20

🏆 Leicester City Player of the Season: 2019–20

🏆 Premier League Golden Boot: 2019–20

VARDY

9 THE FACTS

NAME:
Jamie Richard Vardy

DATE OF BIRTH:
11 January 1987

AGE: 33

PLACE OF BIRTH:
Sheffield

NATIONALITY: England

BEST FRIEND: David 'Nuge' Nugent

CURRENT CLUB: Leicester City

POSITION: ST

THE STATS

Height (cm):	**179**
Club appearances:	**405**
Club goals:	**204**
Club trophies:	**4**
International appearances:	**26**
International goals:	**7**
International trophies:	**0**
Ballon d'Ors:	**0**

★ ★ ★ **HERO RATING: 87** ★ ★ ★

GREATEST MOMENTS

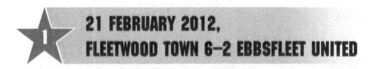

21 FEBRUARY 2012,
FLEETWOOD TOWN 6–2 EBBSFLEET UNITED

Jamie had been making a name for himself in non-
league football for a while, but this hat-trick helped
put him on the radar of Championship clubs like
Leicester City. The goals got better and better: first a
tap-in, then a lovely strike with the outside of his right
foot, and finally, a lob over the keeper from just over
the halfway line.

21 SEPTEMBER 2014, LEICESTER CITY 5–3 MANCHESTER UNITED

In 2014, Jamie helped Leicester to win promotion from the Championship, but was he really good enough to play in the Premier League? He was determined to prove his doubters wrong. So, on his full debut against Manchester United, Jamie led his team to an incredible comeback, setting up four goals and scoring one of his own.

28 NOVEMBER 2015, LEICESTER CITY 1–1 MANCHESTER UNITED

This was the day when Jamie wrote his name in the Premier League history books by becoming the first player to score in eleven consecutive games. Racing through on another classic Leicester counter-attack, Jamie slid his shot past David De Gea to send The Foxes to the top of the table. Six amazing months later, Leicester were crowned Premier League Champions.

4 | 16 JUNE 2016, ENGLAND 2–1 WALES

Jamie had already scored for his country against Germany and the Netherlands, but this one was extra special because it was a crucial goal at Euro 2016. When Hodgson brought him on at half-time, the team were losing 1–0 and in danger of going out of the tournament. But along with Daniel Sturridge, Jamie inspired England to an exciting 2–1 victory.

5 | 4 JULY 2020, LEICESTER CITY 3–0 CRYSTAL PALACE

After a three-month delay due to COVID-19, this was the match when Jamie finally became only the twenty-ninth player to ever score one hundred Premier League goals. It was an amazing achievement, but he didn't stop there. In the last minute, Jamie added a second, taking him to twenty-one goals for the season. Five games later, the Golden Boot was his at last.

PLAY LIKE YOUR HEROES

THE JAMIE VARDY
SPRINT & SHOOT

STEP 1: DON'T. STOP. RUNNING. That's right, you're going to need to be super-fit, as well as super-fast, for this one. When your opponents have the ball, work hard to try to win it back.

STEP 2: Then as soon as your team has the ball again, it's time to turn on your turbo speed boost. ZOOM! Hopefully, your teammates know how to make the most of your pace, and how to play the perfect pass.

STEP 3: Sprint as fast as you can, in between the centre-backs or behind their weakest/slowest defender. Either way, you need to win the race!

STEP 4: As you reach the ball first, it's time to slow down and stay calm. There's no need to get over-excited and rush your shot.

STEP 5: If the goalkeeper decides to dive at your feet, cheekily chip the ball over them. GOAL!

STEP 6: If instead the keeper makes themselves big and tall, aim low, firing an accurate strike into the bottom corner. GOAL!

TEST YOUR KNOWLEDGE

QUESTIONS

1. Who was Jamie's childhood Sheffield Wednesday hero?

2. Who did Wednesday lose to in the FA Cup Final when Jamie went to Wembley?

3. Why did Wednesday decide to let Jamie leave at the age of sixteen?

4. While he was scoring goals for Stocksbridge, what other job did Jamie also do?

5. True or false – Jamie scored three hat-tricks in a row for Halifax Town.

6. How much did Leicester City have to pay Fleetwood Town to sign Jamie in 2012?

7. What number did Jamie get to wear as soon as he arrived at Leicester?

8. Which team did Jamie score his first Premier League goal against?

9. Which country did Jamie score his first England goal against?

10. Whose Premier League goalscoring record did Jamie break in November 2015?

11. What two amazing achievements did Jamie celebrate in July 2020?

Answers below. . . No cheating!

1. David 'Hirsty' Hirst. 2. Arsenal. 3. They said he wasn't big enough to be a top striker. 4. He worked in a factory. 5. False – he got two hat-tricks, but then could only score two goals in the third match. 6. £1 million. 7. Number 9! 8. Manchester United. 9. Germany. 10. Ruud van Nistelrooy. 11. 1) he scored his hundredth Premier League goal and 2) he was awarded the Premier League Golden Boot.

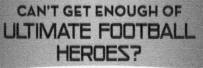

CAN'T GET ENOUGH OF
ULTIMATE FOOTBALL HEROES?

Check out heroesfootball.com
for quizzes, games, and competitions!

Plus join the Ultimate Football Heroes
Fan Club to score exclusive content
and be the first to hear about new
books and events.
heroesfootball.com/subscribe/